The Way Ahead

THE
WAY
AHEAD

Carey Publications Ltd.

ISBN 0 85479 950 8

First printed 1975

Printed by
University Tutorial Press Ltd.
Foxton, near Cambridge, England
for
Carey Publications Ltd.
5 Fairford Close, Haywards Heath,
Sussex RH16 3EF.

CONTENTS

Introduction

THE WORLD WAS ENVELOPED IN SPIRITUAL DARKNESS WHEN JESUS CHRIST was born. Seventy years later light had spread across the world. Starting from Jerusalem churches had been planted in Judea, Samaria and in the main cities of the Mediterranean world. For instance from Ephesus Asia Minor had been evangelized and churches had been planted throughout that whole region. The apostles knew only one way of spreading the light and that was the preaching of the Gospel to the people and the gathering of the converts into local churches.

The world is spiritually dark today and the way to spread the light is the same now as it was at the beginning. We are to preach and evangelize gathering converts into churches in which a New Testament discipline is to pertain.

Yet there are differences between the situation we face and that which applied during the days of the apostles. Much tradition impedes the way though admittedly the obstacles of traditionalism are not more formidable than that of the sheer paganism that confronted the early Christians. How do we forge ahead? Preaching has always been and will always be our chief weapon. Yet it is easy for preaching to fail either in content or in the manner of presentation. Preaching involves the whole counsel of God and this includes the attributes of God. Constant study is essential if preaching is to be worthy of the name.

Evangelism should stem from God's appointed agent, namely, the local church which in turn is nurtured and built up by expository preaching. Why is it that so much evangelism today is ineffective and why is it that revival has disappeared? The chapter on Finney examines these important matters.

Much can be learned from the past and from the life of Calvin Jim van Zyl draws out lessons as to the role of a Pastor. A wide gulf existed between Calvin and the Anabaptists. Nevertheless we ought not to miss some of the lessons which can come from the attempts of the Anabaptists to create gathered churches.

All but one of the chapters which follow are contributed by Carey Conference speakers, but no less than three were delivered at the Annual Evangelical and Reformed Conference of South Africa. Herbert Carson, who is chairman of the Carey Conference, gave his papers on the Attributes of God at Skoegheim in Natal in 1973 and at the same Conference vision of God's chariot-throne moving in irresistible power, and flashing with the light of holiness and judgment, the prophet could go forward with confidence. It is such confidence we need in a day when not only our gospel, but the very concept of preaching is rejected. In a day when the pulpit is denigrated and even evangelicals are tempted to capitulate, preachers need the reassuring awareness that they are men sent by God, the God who, in Paul's words, "works all things after the counsel of his own will".

Our consideration of the attributes of God in relation to the task of preaching must begin with the preacher himself bowing in adoring wonder before the Lord God Almighty. To meet the task of preaching without a deepening knowledge of the Most High is to face the prospect of being crushed by the difficulties and discouragements, or of being destroyed by sinful pride seeking, as it does, for wordly success, which God will reject as wood, hay and stubble, fit only to be consumed by the flames of his judgment.

The preacher then goes to his task as one sent by God, with a message from heaven, depending upon the Holy Spirit to give him the words and the power, aiming to glorify the God whose gospel he expounds. With such a conception of the ministry, there can be no tolerance of suggestions that he should be clever, witty or popular. As an ambassador of the King of kings he is answerable ultimately to his sovereign, and in his words and in the quality of his life he must never forget the God whose commission he bears.

How then, do we preach the attributes of God? How do we set forth in preaching the glory of the God and Father of our Lord Jesus Christ? It should be emphasised from the outset that we must not do so in such a way that the attributes appear as abstractions rather than as the ways in which the living God reveals himself. Clearly, in medicine, there is an important function for the teacher of anatomy who dissects and explains the structure of each bone and each joint; the physiologist who has his role in isolating and describing the functions of the organs of the body. However, the ultimate aim is that the student may build up a coherent picture of a fully integrated and healthy body. Likewise, the attributes of God are not isolated concepts which we string together in our mind to form some overall concept of the divine. We isolate them to study them, but we must be careful to set our studies in the context of a personal knowledge and a living experience of the God who has revealed himself in a variety of ways. There is one God whose unity shines out to us in the diversity of his attributes and we must never lose sight of this unity of essence.

This stress on God's unity will safeguard us against another danger: that of interpreting the attributes of God from the standpoint of a human analogy. In a human personality there is one person, but a variety of

2

human attributes. In man the attributes may clash and cause tension. There may be an over-emphasis of one and an under-emphasis of another. In God there is never a clash, never a competition between one aspect of his being and another. Thus, for example, we must not set his justice against his mercy, as if God faced the inner tensions which can often be so severe for us as we find ourselves pulled in different directions. The essential unity of the Godhead means that there is a harmony in which every aspect of his being, as he reveals himself to us, forms a coherent pattern. The being of God is like a diamond with many facets, which shines brilliantly from whatever side we approach. However, the diamond is not simply the sum total of the facets, nor is God the totality of his attributes. He shines with an undimmed and unchanging glory. Faith approaches, now from this direction and now from that, but always looks beyond the facet under consideration to the essential glory of the God who has condescended to our finite thinking by revealing himself in a diversity which we can consider stage by stage, element by element.

Turning to the general issue of our mode of presenting these truths, we face the fact that preaching is not a stereotyped procedure. The preacher is not a worker in an assembly line, but a craftsman. This means that each sermon will not only bear the stamp of its author, but will have a distinctiveness of approach about it. All preachers worthy of the name are under the direction of the Spirit but, where the Spirit of the Lord is, says Paul, there is liberty. In preaching therefore, while there are spiritual conditions for exercising gifts, there is a freedom in the precise way in which they are exercised. In this issue one man's method is another man's bondage, so we must not be slavish imitators.

In this matter there are basically two approaches; the topical and the expository. I use these terms with hesitation because a man may take a topic and yet root it in solid exegesis. I use the terms simply to contrast the approaches which, in the matter under consideration, would deal with the attributes of God as a subject for a series of sermons, or in the context of continuous exposition of the Word. Shall I, for example, preach on the subject of God's holiness or God's grace or shall I, in the course of general expository preaching, expound these truths as they emerge? My personal preference is for the latter method.

One reason for my approach is that our doctrine of God is not one particular subject within Scripture, but is the background and context of every other truth in Scripture. The Bible is the Word of God. Our basic starting point is that God has spoken. In every word of his revelation his being shines through. To declare what is implied in the revelation in the course of exegetical preaching is to underscore the fact that God's essential being is the context in which his counsel is made known.

There is also the practical issue of the demands of a continuing ministry in one local church. The itinerant preacher may deliver his series to a congregation and move on to deliver it again in a fresh situation, but the pastor who ministers to one congregation faces a different problem. The attributes of God can be classified under a limited number of heads. To expound them thus is to reach the end of the series fairly soon. To return to the same topics at an early date is either to give the impression of the preacher's hobby horse being paraded again, or to introduce, even subconsciously, the feeling that the preacher is just treading a well worn path, or even that he is rather short of ideas! To preach the attributes of God in the course of general exposition is to set them in the context of the Spirit-given variety of the Word. It means that each aspect of God's being is viewed again and again in such varying contexts that the repetition of the theme does not become monotonous, but is, rather, the strong connecting link binding the varied sub-themes of our preaching into a coherent unity. A composer does not aim at monotonous repetition in a symphony. The theme continues to re-appear, but it is within the developing movement of the whole and it both contributes to that development and is itself enhanced by it. To preach the attributes of God in the context of a continuing expository ministry is to discover them as the underlying theme of all we do, throwing light as they do on all the varied aspects of God's truth, and being brought into prominence themselves at the same time.

God has revealed himself in many and varied ways, as the opening statement of Hebrews reminds us. There are his explicit self-disclosures, when in a direct verbal encounter, he makes himself known. Thus to Abraham he declares himself as God Almighty. To Moses he reveals himself as the eternal God, "I AM THAT I AM". He also makes himself known in his actions in history, whether in creation, providence or redemption. "My Father works," says Jesus. He is the God who acts, and in his decisive actions he discloses his being. His actions are not however, bare actions which are susceptible of whatever interpretation we may choose to append to them. God himself interprets his own actions. Biblical revelation is not simply a record of what God has done, but a divinely communicated statement of the significance of his actions. The miracles of Jesus might be to the curious no more than τερατα (wonders) but, inspired by the Spirit, John saw them and presents them as σημεια. Thus, we expound biblical history with a view to disclosing the character and will of the God who has acted in history, either directly or through his providential over-ruling of events. Our exposition of God's own commentary is our attempt to echo the voice which has spoken decisively from heaven through prophet and apostle and, supremely, through the Lord Jesus Christ.

It goes without saying that true preaching is directed to the whole man. The preacher is not simply conveying information, vitally important though the truths are which he preaches. His aim is not a mere orthodoxy in which the acquisition of a doctrinal system is an end in itself. The aim, rather, is so to preach in the power of the Spirit that the Word may be applied to the lives of those who hear. A preacher's desire is to see minds enlightened, consciences probed, hearts moved and wills stirred into action. There is a longing for the sinner to be so overwhelmed with the convicting glimpse of the holiness of God that he will cry for mercy. True biblical preaching will see the saints moved to worship and adoration, to praise and thanksgiving, to glad and willing service, to joyful and consistent witness. The preaching of the attributes of God can be considered in two contexts, that of evangelism and that of worship. Clearly these two are not separate, watertight compartments, for gospel preaching aims to produce worshippers, and a worshipping congregation is itself a potent reinforcement of the gospel which is preached from the pulpit.

Evangelism

We begin with Paul's brief summary of his evangelistic ministry as he speaks to the elders at Ephesus. He had, he claimed, preached persistently, both in public and in private, repentance towards God and faith towards our Lord Jesus Christ. Such an evangelistic message is meaningless, however, apart from a knowledge of the nature of this God towards whom repentance is to be exercised.

Idolatry, as Paul shows in Romans 1, is endemic to human nature. The charge of God in Psalm 50:21 is applicable in every generation and in every individual life: "You thought that I was such a one as yourself." Man constantly fashions a god according to his own ideas. It may be the crudely-carved image of a primitive savage or the figment of the sophisticated imagination of some of our modern theologians; it may be the philosophically conceived absolute of Hinduism or the ill-defined heavenly benevolence of the man in the street—but it is the same pattern, man, the idolater, fashions his own gods.

To launch into a call to repentance and faith is to be in great danger of encouraging man's innate idolatry, whereas the authentic New Testament experience is what the Thessalonians demonstrated: they turned to God from idols to serve the living and true God. One wonders whether the crowds of young people who are precipitated into a decision, which leads to a blind alley or to subsequent rejection of Christianity, have ever been confronted with the true God. To call men to God, without making clear the character of the God to whom they come, is to face the likelihood that they will turn to the god whom they have conceived and so go in a completely false direction.

Indeed, even the term repentance itself has no meaning apart from a knowledge of God. It is possible to stir men's consciences, especially if they have been involved in moral failure, but we may do nothing more than produce a feeling of remorse, or encourage them in the erroneous idea that, if only they can deal with one particular sin and one area of specific moral weakness all will be well. How can they begin to know what

5

repentance really means until they learn what sin is in God's sight? How can they know what sin is, apart from God's law? How can they appreciate the solemn demands of that law and the terrible and eternal consequences of transgressing that law, unless they have some knowledge of the God who has made his demands known?

Man's sorry condition is essentially due to his own self-centred attitude. He is at the centre of his little universe and God is on the periphery to be summoned to man's aid when the occasion demands. The *deus ex machina* of Greek tragedy, the deity who arrives to sort out the problems, is a typically human creation. Man wants God on man's terms. He wants God to give him peace and comfort, but he himself wants to remain at the centre of things. The tragedy of a great deal of evangelical thinking is that it does not deal with this fundamental issue. It tries to interest man by baiting the hook, by showing him the gains which will be his if only he will come to Jesus. It presents Christ as a heavenly psychiatrist waiting to meet our needs. It urges the sinner to be man enough to decide for Christ, thus ensuring that he will come with his pride intact. In short, it makes man the centre, it puts the initiative in his hands, it reduces God to the level of being at man's disposal.

This is certainly not the way to bring men to repentance. It is no wonder that, after generations of this approach, we are in such a morass of superficiality and false profession. The biblical gospel begins with God. It is God who takes the initiative. It is God who saves. Our first task, therefore, is to prise man out of his self-centred state, to deal with his pride, to bring him to his knees before God. Our instrument in this task is the full-orbed doctrine of God. In other words we preach the attributes of God that we may show man in his true condition as a guilty, lost rebel under God's wrath and subject to everlasting judgment. It is only with such a prelude that we can point the awakened sinner to the Christ who delights to show mercy to those who, in repentance, humbly seek him.

We are charged at times that the reformed faith is not evangelistic and, indeed, that by its emphasis on the absolute sovereignty of God it must inevitably stultify evangelistic enterprise, by robbing man of the incentive to act. The very opposite is the case! Encouraging man's initiative is simply encouraging man's pride. To appeal to his desires for this or that benefit is to fail to attack the real citadel, his pride. To begin, on the other hand, with God and to emphasise that man, like all creation, exists only for God's glory is to shatter the self-opinionated humanism of the natural man and to turn his thoughts in the only positive and fruitful direction, that is God-wards.

The biblical account of creation begins with God the Creator, and our gospel preaching must begin there. We are in danger of hurrying so quickly to Mount Calvary that we fail to visit Mount Sinai first. Mount Sinai is only significant, however, when we have first realised that the God whose thunders are heard there is the Almighty Creator of all things and all men. In that classic exposition of the apostolic Gospel the Epistle to the Romans, Paul does not reach his great declaration of the glory of the Cross until late in Chapter 3. First he must establish the reality of man's sin and his consequent guilt. This means he must speak of God's law and this takes him in chapter 1 to the doctrine of Creation.

This approach is seen also in Paul's preaching method. Whether he is preaching to the country folk of Lycaonia or to the intellectuals of Athens he aims to turn them from idolatry and his starting point is the God of Creation who "made heaven and earth, and the sea, and all things that are therein" (Acts 14:15).

To declare that God was "in the beginning" is to embark on the preaching of the divine attributes. He is the one who is prior to time—even to use such a paradoxical phrase is to show how conditioned our minds are to temporal ways. We can think only of the passage of the hours and days and years, but God is the eternal One. The One who was in the beginning is the One who reveals himself as "1 am". (He is not the "I was" or "I will be" but the One who is the eternally present God.) "From everlasting to everlasting, thou art God" (Ps. 90:2). God is the high and lofty One who inhabits eternity (Is. 57:15). "Thou art the same and thy years have no end" (Ps. 102:27). He is the "ancient of days" (Dan. 7:9).

Man in his stupidity and sinfulness lives for time. He behaves as if life were endless. He ignores death and tries to forget it. He forms his plans and pursues his pleasures, all within the confines of time. The Word of God is the Word of the eternal One. It reminds man of the brevity of his life and, indeed, of the brevity of the sum total of human time and human history. The eternal God who inaugurated time and history is the One who will consummate history and terminate time. This is the God with whom we have to do now, and whom we must encounter on the Day of Judgment.

As the eternal God, he is the self-sufficient One. The source of his being is in himself, for, if there were a source beyond him from which his life or being were derived, he would not be God but a creature. Unlike his creatures, however, who all have a derived being, he is himself autonomous and underived. There is no "before", for time is the product of his creative action. We cannot look for a cause or a source prior to God's being, for the very term "prior", with its temporal connotation, has no meaning for One who is eternal. "The Father," says Jesus, "has life in himself" (John 5:26). God "only has immortality" (1 Tim. 6:16). Our life and our immortality are derived from God, the One who was "in the beginning".

The implication of this self-sufficiency of God and this dependence of men is that, God owes nothing to his creatures, while men are completely in

7

debt to him. This was the point Paul made so clearly on Mars Hill. He begins with the "God that made the world" and this leads him to a rejection of idolatry on the ground that God does not require anything from man, seeing that all that man has he has received. It is because God "giveth to all life and breath and all things" that one must conclude that he is not to be "worshipped with men's hands as though he needed anything" (Acts 17:25). To him, then, we owe our life, our being and our existence. On him we depend for the maintenance of the environment, of which the delicately balanced structure makes human life possible. The consequence of all this, as Paul demonstrates in Romans 1, is that man has a responsibility to worship and obey his Creator. Gratitude for the gift of life should lead to a readiness to acknowledge God as the author of all our good, but man has not done this. In fact he has done the opposite. Man has made creation, rather than the Creator, his God.

This, then, is the ugly reality of sin. It is man's rebellion against his Creator. It is the creature shaking his puny fist in defiance in the face of Almighty God. We must stress this point, for there is a danger of leaving men with the false impression that it is particular sins which are their problem. If those particular sins are dealt with, so they think, all will be well. This is far from the case. Particular sins may be dealt with externally by the contact with Christians in a Church fellowship, much as the companionship of Alcoholics Anonymous can break the slavery of drink, but the issue runs much more deeply than this or that specific sin. Indeed, the specific sin is only there because of the underlying sinfulness. We sin because we are sinners. We transgress the law of God because at heart we are rebels. The conviction, therefore, to be aimed at in preaching is this humbling awareness and frank acknowledgment that we are guilty, in that we have taken the lives God has entrusted to us and used them for ourselves.

A further attribute of God comes into view here, to intensify the reality of sin and to magnify its vileness. This God, who has made us for himself, is a holy God. Holiness is one of the attributes most frequently ascribed to God in Scripture. He himself declares, in his demand for holiness among his people, that the reason is, "I am holy" (Lev. 11:44-45; 1 Pet. 1:16). The angels in Isaiah's vision bow in adoring wonder as they sing Holy, holy, holy is the Lord of hosts (Isa. 6:3). The heavenly choir in the Apocalypse worships before the throne of One whose holiness fills them with wonder.

What does the Bible mean by holiness? There is the thought of distinctness, separateness, remoteness even. God is holy in the sense that he is utterly apart from all that is impure, all that is false, all that is sinful. The greatest men have great blemishes and the greater the saint the more aware he is of his own sinful failures. In God there is no flaw, no blemish, no inconsistency. "God is light, and in him is no darkness at all" (1 John 1:5). In God there is utter perfection. Indeed, such is the dazzling glory of his holiness that the reaction of one who glimpses it in some measure is either the prostrate silence of an Ezekiel or a John, or the agonised cry of conviction of an Isaiah.

God's holiness is not, however, some static quality, like one aspect of a portrait. It is, like all his attributes, one way of describing who God is, and how he acts. His holiness is dynamic. It is not only a declaration of his own inherent perfection, but also a declaration of his essential antipathy and antagonism to all that is unholy. He is not apart in the sense of being a remote spectator, viewing from afar an unholy condition which contrasts sharply with his own holiness. He is rather the Judge of all the earth, who demands from men that they should be holy, who assesses their lives by the touchstone of his own holiness and who brings them under his righteous judgment for their sin.

God warns the men of Noah's day, but when they refuse the calls to repentance of the preacher of righteousness the wrath of God overflows in overwhelming judgment. Sodom and Gommorrah may continue apparently unscathed, in spite of their filth, but God's holiness issues in terrible judgment. The self righteousness of the Pharisees may seem to make them immune, but the smoking ruins of Jerusalem in 70 A.D. are both a fulfilment of Jesus' warnings and a reminder that this holy God is not mocked, for "whatsoever a man sows that shall he also reap". The Bible closes with the sombre picture of a doom so terrible that it is presented as a lake of fire which burns day and night for ever and ever.

It is here that our Gospel preaching must begin, as Paul begins in the Epistle to the Romans, with the God who is outraged by the ungrateful rebellion of his creatures and who summons them to judgment. When Paul confronted the Athenian philosophers it was with the divine imperative, "God now commandeth all men everywhere to repent, because he hath appointed a day in which he will judge the world in righteousness by that man whom he hath ordained" (Acts 17:31). In place of a facile, evangelistic approach which tells guilty rebels to "Smile, Jesus loves you", we must begin where the Apostle began: "For the wrath of God is revealed from heaven against all ungodliness and unrighteousness of men." We reject the God-dishonouring approach—which, in fact, is also most damaging to man—which suggests that God is trying to cajole men into accepting Jesus as if he would extract a favour from his own creatures. In its place we preach the judgment of God and the wrath of God. "Our God is a consuming fire." "It is appointed unto men once to die but after this the judgment." In face of the awfulness of such judgment and the clear reminder of Jesus that men should fear him who is able to destroy both body and soul in hell, we call men, not to confer a favour on God, not to open the door and let the rather pathetic figure of their imagination enter, but rather to realise their awful danger and to cry to this holy God that, for Christ's sake, he might have mercy upon them.

9

This holy God is God Almighty. This was the burden of much of the prophets' ministry. They faced the idolatrous idea that Jehovah was simply another Baal, the god of one locality or at best of one nation. Their reply was that he is the Lord of hosts, the God of the nations. In Coverdale's version of Psalm 96:10 there is a wonderful rendering: "Tell it out among the heathen that the Lord is king." God's power is not limited by any conditions to which he is subject. To speak of his omnipotence is to speak in absolute terms and to require no limiting qualifications. He is, in Paul's words, the God "who works all things after the counsel of his own will" (Eph. 1:11).

This means that man is entirely subject to God's sovereign direction and control. Paul uses the Old Testament image of the potter to bring this home. Man, the clay, is in the hands of his Creator and it is folly to try and fight against omnipotence. Of course, man being what he is, his pride will lead him to imagine that he can assert his own autonomy and defy God. The answer to that comes in the vivid words of Psalm 2: "He that sitteth in the heavens shall laugh: the Lord shall have them in derision." The call of the Gospel comes, therefore, from a position of strength, not weakness. The God whom we preach is not looking for man's approval. He commands repentance and the command is reinforced by the assurance that the God who thus commands is the Almighty Judge and, as Hebrews says, "it is a fearful thing to fall into the hands of the living God".

If God is omnipotent, then he is also omnipresent. "Am I a God at hand, saith the Lord, and not a God afar off? Can any hide himself in secret places that I shall not see him? saith the Lord. Do not I fill heaven and earth? saith the Lord" (Jer. 23:23-24). So Adam may hide among the trees of the garden, but God searches him out. Achan may hide his loot, but the eye of God sees all he does. David may conceal his sin from men but not from God. So we get the magnificent statement of Psalm 139. Wherever the Psalmist contemplates flight, God is always there. There is no evading that presence there is no deceiving that scrutiny.

Here is a powerful reinforcement to our Gospel preaching. The sinner is never away from God whose presence is everywhere a reality, and, because God's omnipresence is allied with his omniscience, it is folly for the sinner to try and evade or excuse himself. God's knowledge is not like ours, which is gradually acquired and is always imperfect. God is not learning. There is no new information of which he was formerly ignorant. Because he is eternal, the time process which is basic to human learning has no bearing upon his knowledge. Because he is immutable he cannot grow in knowledge, otherwise he would become what he was not before. Isaiah asks: "Who hath directed the Spirit of the Lord, or being his counseller hath taught him? With whom took he counsel, and who instructed him, and taught him in the path of judgment, and taught him knowledge, and showed to him the way of understanding?" (Isa. 40:13-14).

10

Paul echoes the prophet when he asks in similarly rhetorical fashion, "Who has known the mind of the Lord or who has been his counsellor?" (Rom. 11:34). Hagar, by the well, in Genesis 16, grasped the same truth: he is the God who sees and lives. This means that our hidden thoughts are open to him. The motives behind our actions are patent and obvious to God. Ezekiel, in his vision, was taken into the secret chambers of the temple where men were engaged in abominable practices, but there are no secret places as far as God is concerned. So, we must preach a gospel which follows hard after man and probes the secret places of his heart to expose them to the light of God's holiness. "All things are naked and opened unto the eyes of him with whom we have to do" (Heb. 4:13).

Righteousness is another key word in our Gospel preaching. For men, righteousness means conformity to God's law and obedience to its requirements. When we consider God, however, there is no law to which he is answerable. There is no higher judgment seat to which he may be summoned. The law, after all, is from God; it is itself the expression of God's righteousness. If, then, God cannot be subject to law as to a demand above and beyond himself, in what sense is he to be designated righteous? Surely, in the sense of being consistent with his own character. When he speaks and when he acts he does so in perfect conformity with his own essential being. God's righteousness is his own perfect self-consistency, which is rooted in his immutability. He is the One who changes not (Mal. 3:6). "Thou art the same," sings the Psalmist, "and thy years have no end" (Ps. 102:27).

This means that every suggestion of arbitrariness is ruled out. God is not some capricious deity, moving now this way and now that, he is, says James, "the Father of lights with whom there is no variableness neither shadow of turning" (Jas. 1:17). His law is, therefore, the consistent demand of the consistent God. He will not modify his demands nor will he condone failure. It is because he is righteous that his wrath is revealed from heaven against all ungodliness and unrighteousness of men.

The righteous God is, however, the merciful God. To use the two terms together must not lead to the misconception that they are two competing attributes, as if one aspect of God's being produces a conflict with the other, with a resultant tension and dilemma as far as action is concerned. This is to view God as if he were some kind of super-man with something of man's inconsistency still apparent. God is one, and in the unity of his essence there is no conflict. Indeed, his righteousness, being his self-consistency, embraces his mercy. In his merciful acts he is being consistent with himself; he is being righteous.

It is this righteous mercy which lies behind Paul's exposition of the Gospel in Romans and must undergird our preaching of that Gospel. The death of our representative and substitute, the Lord Jesus Christ, is the reply of God to our sin, for it was God who set him forth as a propitiation.

11

In the exaction of the penalty, the righteous judgment of God is declared and vindicated. In that same moment of judgment God's mercy flows in utter consistency to sinful men.

God's immutability and righteousness lie at the heart of our doctrine of assurance. Our confidence is based on the promises of God. This God is one who has sworn by himself (Heb. 6:13) that he will be faithful to his covenant. So his pledge to his elect, his promises to redeem, keep and glorify, are all guaranteed by his very being. Because he is God, he cannot lie. Because he is God, he will surely perform every word he has spoken and bring every plan he has made to its triumphant consummation. "He who has begun a good work in you will perform it until the day of Jesus Christ" (Phil. 1:6).

All this lifts preaching to a new level. Preachers are not the representatives of a rather spent force, or the spokesmen of an ebbing cause. They are ambassadors of Christ, servants of the Most High God. Their dependence is not on their gifts or persuasive powers, but on the living God, the eternal, almighty, immutable and righteous One. It is the Creator who has commissioned them. It is the Judge of all the earth to whom they are answerable. It is God Almighty who will sustain them. It is the Righteous Redeemer whose evangel we hear. The Devil cannot conquer us. The world cannot destroy us. "The eternal God is our refuge and underneath are the everlasting arms." "The Lord of hosts is with us the God of Jacob is our refuge."

The woman of Samaria and the citizens of Athens had at least one thing in common—they worshipped an unknown God. To the woman Jesus says: "You worship what you do not know," and to the Athenians Paul declares "What therefore you worship as unknown this I proclaim to you". True worship, on the other hand, demands that we know the character of the God we worship. Faith is no blind leap but the trusting response to the Word which God has spoken and which the enlightened understanding has received. Faith comes by hearing and hearing by the Word of God.

What, then, has God said concerning the worship which is acceptable to him? The answer to that question comes in Jesus' words in John 4:24: "God is a spirit: and they that worship him must worship him in spirit and in truth." It must be the true God whom we worship, not an idol of our own making, and our worship must be on the terms which the true God has ordained. The design for the tabernacle did not come from Moses but from God! If, then, we are to be right in the Object of our worship and in the way in which we approach him, we must begin with God's revelation of himself to us. The doctrine of God is the essential pre-requisite for true worship.

The consistent stress of Scripture on right doctrine as the only ground for our approach to God is seen in Paul's reference to singing within the congregation. When we join in psalms, hymns and spiritual songs it is not for the purpose of emotional release, nor to satisfy our desire for good music. It is didactic in aim. "We teach and admonish" one another. The hymn is intended to be not only a song of praise directed to God, but also a means of mutual edification and instruction. Doctrine reigns supreme, not only in the pulpit but when the people sing. Perhaps I should say that doctrine ought to reign there, for often today the songs of the people of God are sadly divorced from biblical truth. However, truth there must be, for if we are to worship God aright we must begin with a knowledge of him, and we must go on to know him more completely until that day when we see him face to face and the knowledge of heaven leads to the perfection of worship.

It is true that, for the Christian, the whole of life should be an act of worship, "Whatever you do in word or deed, do everything in the name of the Lord Jesus giving thanks to the Father through him" (Col. 3:17).

So we may pray with George Herbert:

> Teach me my God and king
> In all things thee to see
> And what I do in anything
> To do it as for thee.

Yet, while there is this general attitude, there are also the special times of worship and the divinely appointed acts of worship. So, while the Psalmist rejoices in the God whose handiwork he sees on every hand, he has a special delight in the sanctuary. "I was glad when they said unto me, Let us go into the house of the Lord" (Ps. 122:1). "How lovely is thy dwelling place O Lord of hosts! My soul longs, yea faints for the courts of the Lord. A day in thy courts is better than a thousand" (Ps. 84:1, 2, 10). This note is carried over into the New Testament. When Paul tells the Corinthians that they are the temple of the Holy Spirit the very term he uses indicates that one important aspect of their corporate life is that they are a worshipping fellowship. The directions of the New Testament epistles for regulating worship point in the same direction. Whether it is the reference to the singing in the assembly in Colossians or Ephesians, or the control of abuses at Corinth, or the warnings against discrimination in the epistle of James, the constant presupposition is that, on the Lord's Day, the people of God will gather together to hear the Word, to pray, to sing and to break bread. Indeed, the very essence of the Lord's supper is the pre-supposition of a gathered community sharing together in the common meal of the faithful.

At this point we must look at the relationship between preaching and worship. Two extremes may be noted here. There are those for whom the sermon is secondary, so much so that it can become an optional extra, to be dispensed with if need be. With an open Bible before us we

13

are hardly likely to succumb to such a designation of the ministry of the Word! Among the Reformed, however, there is a danger of the other extreme, in that the worship is viewed as a mere prelude to the preaching. Thus, in some circles, the worship of the people of God is designated by that derogatory title "the preliminaries".

Surely the biblical position is at neither of these extremes. The ministry of the Word is of vital significance and nothing must be allowed to detract from the importance of the pulpit, but the preaching is in the context of a worshipping congregation. Indeed, one must surely insist that preaching itself is worship. The preacher's task is not simply to lecture, and certainly not to entertain, but to direct men's minds and hearts God-wards. The preacher exercises his ministry as in the presence of God and in those moments of true freedom in the pulpit when he knows the power of the Spirit, he feels himself caught up into fellowship with the God whose glory he is aiming to declare.

Furthermore, it is to a people bowed in worship that the message comes with power. Congregations vary greatly and their impact upon the preacher can be marked. There are times when an unprepared, inattentive, and unresponsive people can chill the soul of the most passionate preacher. There are, thank God, congregations whose openness to the Word and adoring response to God's revelation will lift an ordinary preacher to extraordinary heights.

The corollary is also true. If the congregation can make or mar the preaching, then it is also a fact that the preaching moulds the congregation. There is an element of inter-dependence here. Hence it is, on the one side, the worshipping congregation which is the context for and the stimulus to good preaching and, on the other side, faithful and consistent preaching which nourishes and builds up such a congregation. The pulpit, therefore, is to be seen as the source from which the congregation draws both its incentive for worship and also its instruction as to how that worship is to be offered. The response of a grateful congregation is to bring a readiness of mind and heart, so that the preacher is himself stirred to measure up to their demands. Together they learn from the Word of God and together they are drawn out to God in praise, thanksgiving and adoring worship.

This means that the attitude of the people of God at prayer will be deeply influenced by that of the minister in the pulpit. Later we shall be considering the content of his preaching and the effect it should have, but we must begin with his own approach, for the congregation's response to the ministry will be coloured by what seems to them to be the preacher's own attitude. The current trend in some quarters, with its flippancy, jokes and its attempts to entertain is hardly likely to elicit from the hearers an answering response of reverence and awe. It is when the preacher is himself so aware of the majesty and glory of God, and when his own sinfulness and indebtedness to grace are vividly before his mind, that he will preach with a due sense of the solemnity of the task, and such a reverent approach in the pulpit will indicate to those in the pew how men ought to hear God's word and how they ought to respond. I am not suggesting of course, some kind of pulpit manner with a cultivated pseudo-seriousness—this is simply a form of ecclesiastical affectation! Nor am I saying that God's gift of humour is suspect—one imagines that a smile appeared at some of Spurgeon's sallies—but it is one thing to reinforce the truth in what may be a spontaneously humorous fashion and quite another to try and create an atmosphere by the homiletical wise-crack. It is worse to strive for an effect which will focus attention on the preacher's ability rather than the grace of God.

The preacher must convey to his hearers from the outset the impression that all he does and says is subject to the Word of God. In some Presbyterian churches this has been visually indicated by the tradition of having the pulpit Bible carried before the minister into the pulpit. The older Anglican evangelicalism had the same kind of emphasis when they insisted that the lectern should be in a central position. We may not feel drawn in the direction of that kind of symbolism, but certainly we should exhibit the attitude which those symbols were intended to convey, namely the subjection of both preacher and people to the Word of God.

Turning now to the more particular issues of the content of preaching in its relation to worship, we begin with what seems to me to be a fundamental assertion, namely that biblical worship is Trinitarian in its structure. Paul gives a succinct summary of this in Ephesians 2:18: "Through him (Christ) we both have access by one Spirit unto the Father." The Holy Spirit is the controller and director of our worship. The Lord Jesus Christ is the mediator and the goal is the Father's presence.

There are ominous signs in Evangelical circles today that we need, with renewed emphasis, to preach the doctrine of the Trinity. The "Jesus" of much that is current today has almost ousted the Father from the thinking and, noticeably, from the praying of those who profess to be Bible Christians. The Jesus of the New Testament is quite insistent that his aim is to lead men not simply to himself but to the Son. Listen, however, to some of the praying among young people today and one will notice an over-emphasised approach to the Father. The same is true in the teaching of children, who are encouraged to pray to Jesus as if the Father scarcely existed.

Let me make it quite plain that I do not reject prayer addressed to the Lord Jesus Christ nor, for that matter, direct invocation of the Holy Spirit, for both are to be found in the New Testament. Stephen, in his hour of testing, prays, "Lord Jesus receive my spirit". Saul on the Damascus Road asks the risen Christ for instruction as to what he is to do. In 1 Timothy 1:12 Paul thanks Christ Jesus for the grace which saved

15

him. So, too, apart from the invocation of the Spirit in baptism and in the Benediction, a comparison of Matthew 9:38 and Acts 13:4 would suggest that the Spirit is the One who sends the missionaries and who, therefore, may be invoked to send forth labourers into his harvest. However, what I am concerned to do is to stress the balance of Scripture and to indicate the normal pattern of prayer as it appears in the New Testament, in which the Father is the object of prayer and praise. Apart from the obvious example of the Lord's prayer, there is the prayer meeting of Acts 4:24, the prayer of Paul in Ephesians 3:14, with its strong Trinitarian emphasis, the prayers of Philippians 1:3; Colossians 1:3 and 1 Peter 1:3. There is also the stress in Hebrews on the high priesthood of Jesus Christ, which means that through him we go with boldness to the Father. The ascription of praise in Revelation 1:6 is to Christ who has made us kings and priests unto God and his Father.

This in no way relegates Christ to some peripheral place in our worship. He remains central, for in him the Father has made himself known to us —"He that hath seen me hath seen the Father". Through him, as mediator, we draw near to the Father and, since there is no other way of approach, we honour the One who is our all-sufficient advocate—we glory in Christ because "if any man sin, we have an advocate with the Father, Jesus Christ the righteous: and he is the propitiation for our sins" (1 John 2:2). We must not lose sight of the Trinitarian emphasis, however, which in the economy of redemption focuses attention on the mediatorial work of the Son. Hebrews 13:15 urges us: "Through him (Christ) then let us offer the sacrifice of praise to God continually, that is, the fruit of our lips that acknowledge his name!"

Nor does this belittle the rôle in worship played by the Holy Spirit. It is, after all, due to his regenerating work that there is a worshipping community at all. It is his continuing work of conviction and rebuke which leads to a spirit of penitence. It is his enlightenment of our minds which enables us to grasp the truths of Scripture and respond to them in believing worship. It is the Spirit who glorifies Christ (John 16:14) it is by his aid alone that we are able to say "Jesus is Lord" (1 Cor. 12:3). It is in the One Spirit that we come to the Mediator and through him to the Father (Eph. 2:18). True prayer is prayer in the Holy Spirit (Jude 20), and in the deepest exercise of the soul it is the Spirit who makes intercession for us with groanings which cannot be uttered (Rom. 8:26). In short, if we are to worship aright we must be prepared by the Holy Spirit, and if we are to understand and apply the biblical principles of worship it is the Spirit who must teach us and enable us to obey.

How, then, shall we approach the triune God? To this we add an allied question: how shall we preach so that our approach may be in spirit and in truth? Our answer must begin with a basic element in the doctrine of God: the divine sovereignty. God is not answerable to anyone outside himself. To the man who insists on probing into the inner counsels of the Godhead he says: "Who art thou that repliest against God?" Faced with the assertion of absolute sovereignty the pride of man rebels and rejects the idea out of hand, but the believing soul bows in adoration and humble submission. Because God is sovereign, I dare not dictate my mode of approach to him. King Uzziah in the Old Testament provides a sobering reminder of the presumption which God rejects and judges. I will set up my tabernacle, but it must be according to the pattern which the Sovereign Lord prescribes. Worship is not to be governed by considerations drawn from the expertise of the psychologist, nor from the wisdom of the world, but by the principles laid down by the Sovereign Lord himself. He is the true God to whom alone worship is due and "his truth" declares the way in which this God must be approached.

One of the most characteristic phrases in Scripture is "the glory of God". God's glory is the shining forth, the manifestation, the disclosure of his essential excellence. He is the God of majesty and power. His transcendence raises him high above the creation which owes its being to the high and lofty One. What should be the response of the creature to such a revelation of the divine glory? Surely it should evoke awe and reverence and godly fear. It is significant that the Epistle to the Hebrews, which so emphasises the boldness with which we may approach the throne, also stresses the reverence and godly fear with which we should draw near to the consuming fire.

This sense of reverence and awe contrasts sharply with the approach which has become all too common. A glib, free-and-easy attitude is encouraged. Biblical boldness is perverted into cheap familiarity. The joy which should characterise Christians at prayer degenerates into heartiness or, worse still, flippancy. Irreverence is accepted and excused. This is noticeably prevalent in youth rallies where it seems to be assumed that a special approach is required. Yet does God cease to be God because of the age group involved? Are we to substitute for the God of glory a projection of the mentality conditioned by the entertainment industry? When the Psalmist calls us to make a joyful noise it is with an attitude of reverence. "Let us worship and fall down, let us kneel before the Lord our maker." The early believers in the Acts of the Apostles had learnt the lesson. Fresh from the outpouring of the Spirit at Pentecost and rejoicing with a joy unspeakable and full of glory, they yet avoid completely the off-hand or casual approach so beloved today. Instead they begin their prayer meeting with an awareness of the sovereignty of God.

Closely allied to God's sovereignty is his work of creation. We have seen how basic the doctrine of creation is to our evangelism. It is equally basic to our worship. It is not only that the glory of his handiwork should stir us, it is that his majesty and power are so manifest in his work that we bow in praise and submission. It is possible, after all, to be deeply moved by a glorious sunset or a beautiful landscape without there being any element of worship. Indeed, there is an even greater danger in that

17

we may mistake aesthetic appreciation for true worship. One sees this in the sense of wonder evoked by such a building as King's College Chapel in Cambridge. This wonder is not worship, it is simply one more piece of evidence that man was made in the image of God and, though he has sadly defaced that image, there is still in him the capacity to respond to beauty. However, worship, despite creation's beauty, is no mere aesthetic response, nor is it the blurred mysticism of a pantheistic interpretation of reality. If it is to be true worship it must emerge from a robust theism which distinguishes between the Creator and his creation and, seeing the beauty and glory of the latter, looks beyond in adoration to the surpassing glory of the Lord of creation himself.

The beauty of creation is, after all, only a finger pointing heavenwards. The source of creation's loveliness is God himself. Beauty may not be an attribute which we ordinarily apply to God but it is certainly so applied in Scripture. The Psalmist's prayer is "that I may dwell in the house of the Lord all the days of my life, to behold the beauty of the Lord and to enquire in his temple" (Ps. 27:4). When he sings "how lovely is thy dwelling place", he does not stop short with the beauty of the temple but looks beyond to the beauty of God. God's beauty is the harmony of his attributes, the symmetry of his actions and the appropriateness of all his deeds.

When Jesus spoke of himself as the good shepherd he used the epithet καλος, which has the notion not only of moral goodness, but also of beauty. The Platonic idea το καλον embraced in one concept the good, the true and the beautiful, so in Christ goodness, truth and beauty blend together. No wonder, then, that God's people have found the Song of Solomon an appropriate vehicle for devotion, as it speaks of him who is altogether lovely (Song 5:16). No wonder that Samuel Rutherford could write so feelingly as he does in his letters of the loveliness of Christ. Such beauty which, because of our limited vision and our sin-darkened minds, we can but glimpse from afar, should stir us with an aesthetic appreciation which becomes adoring worship. The call of the Psalmist is appropriate: "Worship the Lord in the beauty of holiness" (Ps. 29:2). So Faber bids us sing:

> My God, how wonderful Thou art
> Thy majesty how bright!
> How beautiful Thy mercy-seat,
> In depths of burning light!

> How wonderful, how beautiful,
> The sight of Thee must be,
> Thine endless wisdom, boundless power,
> And awful purity!

The almighty and omniscient God is not only the Lord of creation, but the God of providence. Though he is beyond time, he yet controls time.

Transcending the events of history, he yet directs history. Christian theism is far removed from deism or from the fatalistic aloofness of an Islamic deity. Our God is at once transcendent and immanent, at once far off and near at hand, exalted above the heavens, yet present in every place.

The sweep of history is under his control so that Cyrus emerges on the scene at the moment when Jeremiah's prophecy is ready for fulfilment; Augustus Caesar calls for the census which brings Joseph and Mary to Bethlehem as Micah foretold. Even the apparently minute events have their place—the crowing of a cock falls into the pattern of redemption history. Seeming chance occurrences are not excluded—a man lets fly an arrow with no particular target in view, but the hand of divine justice guides it unerringly to Ahab. "The lot is cast into the lap," says Proverbs 16:33, "but the whole disposing thereof is of the Lord". Indeed, the evil deeds of men are still subject to that sovereign control. Joseph's brothers acted from jealousy and bitterness, but later they were reminded: "You meant evil against me but God meant it for good!" (Gen. 50:20). It was not they who brought Joseph into Egypt, but God (Gen. 45:8). This is seen supremely at the cross. Judas's treachery was his own and the Jewish leaders stood condemned for their sin, but God took both and used them, and Pilate too, as his unwitting instruments. So, says Peter, "Him being delivered by the determinate counsel and foreknowledge of God ye have taken and by wicked hands have crucified and slain" (Acts 2:23). God always stands supreme!

Preaching, then, should call the people of God to reflect on his providence. The call of Deuteronomy is still a valid one: "Thou shalt remember all the way the Lord thy God hath led thee." We must echo the reminder of Christ, that the very hairs of our head are all numbered and that the God, who watches the sparrow fall, watches over his people. "The eyes of the Lord are upon the righteous, and his ears are open unto their cry" (Ps. 34:15). Divine power and wisdom, allied to love and mercy, plot the course for the child of God. To preach the providence of God, not in some abstract fashion, but in the context of the warm covenant relationship between God and his people, is to call out from them an answering response of praise. "I will bless the Lord at all times: his praise shall continually be in my mouth. O magnify the Lord with me, and let us exalt his name together" (Ps. 34:1, 3). Such praise also leads to the quiet confidence which adds the dimension of serenity and tranquil assurance to our worship. To know that the faithful God is at work, and that he is carrying out an eternal plan, is to enter into a deepening experience of the peace of God. A congregation nourished on such preaching will, in its corporate enjoyment of God's peace, both glorify the Lord and exercise a healing ministry to those members who are under the severe pressures of life, or are casualties of the tensions which are constantly present with all of us.

Fear Him ye saints and you will then
Have nothing else to fear.
Make but His service your delight
Your wants shall be His care.

The holiness of God, which is the constantly recurring theme in gospel preaching, never ceases to be a dominant theme as ministers aim to impart to God's people his whole counsel. Not only are men and women called to faith in Christ, who is the way to the Father; not only are they summoned to worship with the assurance of the adopted sons and daughters of God, so that they can say with confidence "Our Father". They are also directed to Jesus' own prayer in John 17, where he uses the ascription "Holy Father". So the God who has made us, redeemed us and adopted us never ceases to be the Holy One. Nor must our assurance and confidence lead us to ignore the implications for worship of his holiness.

The first and obvious response is an awareness of our own sinfulness. "Who among us shall dwell with the devouring fire? who among us shall dwell with everlasting burnings?" (Is. 33:14). This means that there must be a strongly penitential note in our worship, as we come afresh to ask for forgiveness. Paradoxical though it may seem to the outsider, this grief of soul over sin, this shame at personal failure, is suffused with praise and thanksgiving, for the realisation of our sin is at the same time the realisation of the glorious truth that the blood of Jesus Christ cleanses us from all sin. Thus, we reject the charge that preaching the holiness of God and the sinfulness of man can lead to a morbid condition. On the contrary, it is the only way towards a true joyfulness. The so-called joy of a meeting in which men are not made aware of their sin is a mere stirring of the emotions, which cannot last and will, indeed, lead to a great disillusionment. The great hymns of praise in which the wonder of God's pardon is extolled and the power of Christ's cleansing blood declared, spring from hearts which know their own wickedness. Such knowledge arises as we contemplate the One who is Holy.

Some of those who gather for worship may be doing routine jobs which have a deadening effect upon the soul. For others, the small world of suburbia with its inconsequential trivialities is their normal habitat. How can they be lifted from the trivial, the petty, the commonplace, into an awareness of their heavenly calling; how can ministers show them the glory of the heavenly places in which they dwell? Surely it is by preaching the eternity of God. The everlasting God is concerned with the details of our living. He does not ignore the boring, repetitive jobs in which some of his people are involved. He sees the restricted context in which some lives are cast. He is the eternal One, and his people can lift their eyes from the temporary and passing pattern to the expansive magnitude of eternity. The awe and wonder, the sense of the greatness and eternity of God, these will lift us from the rut and show us our true destiny as the pilgrim church on the way to glory.

The eternity of God is also a truth which bears upon our evangelistic and missionary concern and, so, will affect the intercession for the work of the gospel. The God whose glory we preach is not producing hastily devised remedies to meet a deteriorating situation, he is not improvising, as we do because our plans have not developed in the way we hoped. He is the eternal God who has a purpose, whose outworkings transcend time and space. To those chosen in Christ before the foundation of the world it is made clear that this gospel of the kingdom shall be preached among all the nations, that the earth shall be filled with the knowledge of the glory of God as the waters cover the sea, that Jesus Christ shall reign for ever and ever. Thus, faith is kindled and hope renewed. We are not a spent force nor a lost cause, we are the servants of the most high God. Our prayer, then, is no despairing cry but the confident committal to him of the outcome of his purposes, which he will surely perform. Prayer bursts into praise as we realise that our praying and our testimony are elements in that eternal purpose and that we are parts, small but significant, in a purpose which has its roots in the eternal God and which he will inevitably bring to a great consummation.

Furthermore, God is love! The God of sovereign might, majesty and holiness, is the One whose love has shone with inextinguishable glory in the face of Jesus Christ. That love has been displayed at Calvary, in the incredible fact that it was for the ungodly that Christ died. It has been shown to those same ungodly ones, in that God has made us his own sons by adoption. So John, with a deep sense of wonder, writes, "See what love the Father has given us that we should be called children of God; and so we are" (1 John 3:1).

This love of God is no isolated attitude. To treat it thus is to end in the shallow sentimentality of those who forget his holiness and his wrath. "God is love" says John, but he has already said "God is light and in him is no darkness at all". We preach the love of God in all its fulness, but we do so within the context of his other attributes. To do so is not to qualify his love or to make it appear less than it really is. On the contrary, it is to magnify it, for the love of God is not like one man's affection for another, a reaction easily explained. It is rather the love of an infinitely holy One for an abysmally sinful one, and such a love not only defies our powers of description, but transcends our ability to comprehend. The adoring soul beholds that love and is lost in wonder, love and praise.

Worship, I maintained at the outset, is Trinitarian in its structure, and so in our approach to the Throne we never lose sight of the Mediator through whom we come. He is the Son of God, the second person of the blessed Trinity. Hence, what we postulate of God the Father we also ascribe to God the Son. Behind the miracle of the incarnation, the atoning death, the resurrection and ascension, we behold the glory of the only begotten of the Father. He is no creature of time, not even, as the Jehovah's Witness tries to assert, the first creature. He is the eternal One. "In

21

the beginning was the Word, and the Word was with God, and the Word was God" (John 1:1). So, when John on the island of Patmos was given a vision of the ascended Christ, he was overwhelmed. The Christ he saw was one like a son of man, clothed with a long robe and with a golden girdle round his breast, his head and his hairs were white as white wool, white as snow; and his eyes were like a flame of fire; his feet were like burnished bronze, refined as in a furnace; and his voice was like the sound of many waters; in his right hand he held seven stars, from his mouth issued a sharp two edged sword, and his face was like the sun shining in full strength. It is no surprise to us that John describes his reaction: "I fell at his feet as though dead." How far removed is this from the contemporary approach to Jesus! Can one conceive John calling on his fellow believers to give a cheer for Jesus? Even to mention such an idea is to show how grotesquely inappropriate it is.

The great hymn writers of the Church of God did not react in this way. "Thou art the everlasting Son of the Father" wrote the author of that early Christian hymn the *Te Deum*. Charles Wesley speaks in hushed tones of

> Our God contracted to a span
> Incomprehensibly made man.

Josiah Conder summons us to reverent worship:
> Worthy O lamb of God art thou
> That every knee to thee should bow.

It is this same awareness that the One who died at Calvary was the infinite and eternal God which prompted Charles Wesley to cry in questioning gratitude:
> Amazing love! how can it be
> That thou my God shouldst die for me?

Christ, then, is the very centre of the worshipping fellowship, for the attributes of God shine out to us in the glory of the incarnate One. "No man has seen God at any time," says John, and if we were left to our own speculation we would grope interminably in the twilight of our own guesswork. However, the God of grace has not left us in this uncertainty, he has spoken to us in Christ. The only begotten Son, who is in the bosom of the Father, he has declared him.

To return to the text with which we began—through Christ we have access in one Spirit to the Father—we must also keep before us the part played by the Holy Spirit in our knowledge of God. It was he who moved holy men of God to write the Scriptures, in which God is revealed to us. It is he who enlightens our minds to understand the Scriptures. The objective revelation and the inward testimony are both required if we are to know God. By his accomplishment in us of the miracle of the new birth, he has brought us into the fellowship of the people of God. "You are the temple of the Holy Spirit," says Paul, and Peter reminds us in 1 Peter 2:9 that the purpose of this call is that we might declare the wonderful deeds of him who called us out of darkness into his marvellous light.

The implications of these truths for the subject under consideration are plain. The preaching which aims to declare the glory of God must be under the sovereign direction of the Holy Spirit, and the worship of those who receive the Word must also be subject to the Spirit's control. Since the Holy Spirit uses the Scriptures as his instrument, we are simply saying that the standard by which both preacher and hearer are judged, the criterion for assessing both preaching and worship, is the Spirit-given and Spirit interpreted Word of God.

The practical bearing of all this should also be apparent. The preacher must not only be taught by the Spirit, he must seek to be filled with the Spirit if he is to measure up to the exacting standards of the Apostle: "My speech and my preaching was not in enticing words of man's wisdom, but in demonstration of the Spirit and of power" (1 Cor. 2:4). Or again: "Our gospel came not unto you in word only, but also in power, and in the Holy Ghost and in much assurance" (1 Thess. 1:5). Preachers are not simply to be advocates presenting a carefully prepared case, important though that aspect of preaching is; they are to be witnesses filled with the Holy Spirit, so that with assurance they can echo the confidence and authority of the Master himself: "We speak of what we know and bear witness to what we have seen" (John 3:11).

The terms used in Scripture for worship are expressive of the attitude which the redeemed sinner should adopt before his Lord. In the Old Testament there is the Hebrew word צֲבוֹדָה which is the performance of an צֶבֶד a servant. In Exodus 21:1-6 we see, in the ritual used for the retention of the slave who does not wish to leave his master, that the ideal servant is a willing one and, indeed, the glory of the suffering servant of Jehovah in Isaiah's prophecy is that he gladly went to do Jehovah's bidding. Two words are used by the Septuagint to translate the word re-appear in the New Testament, λατρεία and λειτουργία. In both cases the idea of service is present—the latter word was in fact used in a secular sense of service to the state, but is employed with a religious connotation for the worship of the servant of God (Phil. 2:17, 30; Heb. 8:6, 9:21). The cognate verb λειτουργέω seen, for example, in Acts 13:2 conveys the same thought.

Another Old Testament word is the Hebrew verb שָׁחָה, meaning to bow down. So, in Genesis 24:52 Abraham's servant bows earthwards and in 2 Chronicles 7:3 the children of Israel prostrate themselves with faces to the pavement. The Septuagint translaters use the term προσκυνέω which is frequently employed by the New Testament writers. This word suggests the idea of deep reverence, humility and submission.

23

The very language of worship thus implies the doctrine of God. The slave before his master, the adoring worshipper prostrate before the Lord—these figures are appropriate in the context of the revelation of the God of glory. It is because of the glory and majesty of his being, the greatness of his power, the wonder of his condescending mercy and grace that we respond in praise, worship and glad submission. Thus, the worship of the people of God turns their hearts heavenwards and then sets their feet to go at his bidding and to live to his praise and glory. Philip Doddridge puts it superbly.

> "My gracious Lord I own Thy right
> To every service I can pay;
> And call it my supreme delight
> To hear Thy dictates and obey!"

THE MINISTER AND THE DISCIPLINE OF STUDY

Geoff Thomas

I HEARD THE PREACHER, AND GREW INCREASINGLY RESTLESS AS CLANGING cliché and folksy anecdote provided all the tell-tale signs of last-minute preparation. I heard another and was equally ill-at-ease as point after sub-point after sub-sub-point was sonorously intoned, devoid of all application, crushing all interest, and displaying again that absence of discipline in preparation which results in the study being brought into the pulpit and the chapel being turned into the lecture-room.

I could see myself too clearly in these men.

There is scarcely a greater need than that ministers should give themselves to the true discipline of study. The subject will be opened up in the following way.
1. *The Necessity of Study*
2. *The Consequence of Study*
3. *The Need for Discipline*
4. *The Means of Discipline.*

1. The Necessity of Study

History shows us the influence of great ideas. Nothing is as powerful as an idea whose time has come; then it is that men's minds are gripped, their imaginations fired and their devotion captured. Today, most of the world is captured by the ideologies of men, and we are confident that it is to be conquered by Christ. What sort of conquest will that be? It is certainly not a crusade with force of arms, but the operation of God's truth brought to bear by the Spirit on all nations of men, for the weapons of our warfare are not carnal, but mighty through God to the pulling down of strongholds, casting down imaginations, and every high thing that exalteth itself against the knowledge of God, and bringing every thought into the obedience of Christ (2 Cor. 10:4, 5). The Christian cannot rest, Paul says, while a single thought of a single man is not acknowledging the Lordship of Christ. This is the most momentous battle of ideas, as the truth of God overthrows the lies of men. The church cannot afford to have a single member failing to use his mind and not disciplining himself in the study of the Word of God. Has not God made us in his image, and is not one implication of that our ability to study? See how the Psalmists contrast men with animals; Be ye not as the horse, or as the mule, which have no understanding (Ps. 32:9). So foolish was I, and ignorant: I was as a beast before thee (Ps. 73:22). The inference is clear, to fail to use one's mind is to deny the image of God in us. The great indictment we lay upon sinners today is simply that they do not think. Conversation dies where cheap literature, the public house and continuous entertainment *via* radio and T.V. hold sway. Even highly educated men become unthinking, like animals. Where do men discuss the great issues of life, death and eternity? We hear them not. Their understandings are darkened and they mind the things of the flesh. An unthinking man is a sinful man, because he is denying the fact that he is made in the image of God. Again, has not God made a universe in which everything indicates it comes from his hands because it is orderly and capable of our understanding? Day unto day uttereth speech (not a babble) and night unto night sheweth knowledge (not ignorance) (Ps. 19:2). Scientific progress is only possible because of the creation. The general revelation of God is essentially rational and so too is God's special, redemptive revelation. There has been given to us a body of doctrine, a definite positive teaching which claims to be true and exposes falsehood. The Christian gospel is based upon knowledge, and whenever that glorious revelation of truth that longs to ransack our hearts and minds and fill them with the unsurpassable excellencies of the covenant of grace becomes emptied of its doctrinal content then men's religion becomes insipid and unsatisfactory. Again, all Christians should use their minds, because that salvation which comes by the proclamation of the gospel addresses men's minds and renews God's image in man. Paul tells the Colossians, Put on the new man which is renewed in *knowledge* after the image of him that created him (Cols. 3:10). A result of regeneration is that men begin to think aright for the first time about the creation and about themselves. He that is spiritual judgeth all things, he has the mind of Christ.

So, to fail to study, or to encourage anything which denigrates the mind is to undermine the place God has given to this both in creation and redemption. Has God created us in his image and dare we deny the humanity he has given us? Has God spoken to us and shall we not listen carefully to every word of his? Has he renewed our minds in knowledge and shall we not use them to his glory? Is it not our lament today that there are people in our congregations who simply do not use their minds and never read a Christian book? We cry with Hosea, My people are destroyed for lack of knowledge (Hos. 4:6). The Lord says, Because thou hast rejected knowledge I will also reject thee—God actively judges an ignorant church. It is not a matter of luxury whether we use our minds aright or not, all Christians must know the need to resist wandering thoughts when it comes to the reading and studying the Word.

Ministers of the gospel have a special responsibility to apply themselves to study. We could not make that statement if the whole function of the minister was inspirational. If our task was to rouse our congregations to action and set their religious emotions surging then we would have no special calling to study, but if, as Warfield says, the minister is the mouthpiece of the Most High, charged with a message to declare, expound and enforce, standing in the name of God before men and making known to them who and what this God is and what his purposes of grace are and what is his will for his people, then all that is changed. The prime duty of the minister is to know God's message which has been committed to him for the people and to know it thoroughly, so that he can preach it with confidence and exactness. He must be able to know the truth of God with understanding, urge it with authority, defend it with skill and build up men by means of it into a true knowledge of God and of his will, so that however fiercely their faith is assaulted they will stand. As that is so, no second-hand knowledge of God will be sufficient to convey and apply these truths to men from the moment they are converted until the time they are presented perfect to God. For this task the most complete wisdom of the world is useless. Nothing is sufficient for it but to *know*—to know the Book, to know it at first hand, and to know it through and through. So all the discipline of study must be brought to bear upon it.

There are those who say that the simple gospel is enough and we may, with Warfield, thank God that the gospel is simple and is enough, but it is not a simple matter properly to apply this simple gospel to folk in all their varied relations and in the multitude of dilemmas that arise in the entanglements of the twentieth century. Nor has there ever been a time when the exposition and application of the gospel to men and women was a simple matter. The letter to the Romans is the right exposition of the gospel; for eleven chapters Paul works it out in wonderful detail. He was not misguided into thinking that the gospel was so simple that Roman Christians could be left to themselves to work it out, nor was it so simple that it did not need an apostle to explain it properly!

27

Of course the simple preaching of the simple gospel will not fail in its effect. A child lovingly may lisp the name of Jesus and a man be converted, but that is no reason why we should fill our pulpits with children lisping the name of Jesus. The foolishness of preaching is one thing, foolish preaching is another. It is the same in preaching as in everything else—knowledge is power. Nothing can supersede the necessity of knowledge—fervour cannot, devotion cannot, zeal cannot. Yes, knowledge without zeal is useless, but zeal without knowledge is worse than useless, it is destructive. Warfield asks; "why was William Farel, consumed with zeal, burning with evangelical fervour, proclaiming the pure gospel, helpless at Geneva—until with dreadful imprecations he brought to his aid John Calvin, scholar become saint, scholar-saint become preacher of God's grace?"[1]

Knowledge is absolutely indispensable for the minister of the gospel, and nothing is more harmful than to set knowledge and godliness over against one another. Football coaches do not argue whether it is better for a forward to have a right leg or a left leg! He needs both. There are those who say that ten minutes on one's knees will give a truer, deeper knowledge of God than ten hours over one's books. We reply, Why not ten hours over one's books on one's knees? Why should one turn *from* God when one turns *to* one's books? Or turn *from* one's books in order to turn *to* God? If studying is antagonistic to the spiritual life then the whole intellectual life is accursed and there is no question of the possibility of a religious life for the minister. Yet this is the inevitable conclusion of one strand of evangelicalism; hear for example the impassioned utterance of C. T. Studd; "God wants faith and fools, not talent and culture. It is the hot free heart and not the balanced head that knocks the devil out. Ours not to reason why; ours but to dare and dash forward". Stirring stuff no doubt, but perilous because it creates tensions and suspicions where the Bible sees none. Why not warm hearts *and* balanced heads? Being a minister does not free a man from the discipline of study, it drives him to study with devotion.

Teach me my God and King in all things Thee to see
And what I do in anything to do it as for Thee.

Those last words are the great theme of Christian discipleship—"for thy sake". Whether it is the Christian nurse cleaning the pus and matter from a festering wound, the daughter laying aside the hope of marriage to care for an elderly mother, or the minister checking a concordance for the references, and then the dictionaries and lexicons for the nuance of meaning of a word, or familiarising himself with the origins and teachings of contemporary cults, or whatever laborious task it is, he does it "as for thee". This is the doctrine of vocation; God lays upon us all a certain work and whatever we do is done heartily as to the Lord. Charles Hodge, speaking of Philip Lindsay, the most popular professor in Princeton in the last century, says: "he told our class that we would find that one of the

28

best preparations for death was a thorough knowledge of the Greek grammar!" Hodge adds that this was his way of telling us that we ought to do our duty. Of course it is a serious matter if anyone neglects his duty; we are swift to remind our congregations and our children of their responsibility in their vocations. So it is with ourselves; we can build up a religious life only by performing simple duties faithfully.

Ministers cannot avoid the duties of study because of this prime fact; the Bible was given by God in Greek and Hebrew. It is this word as originally given which alone is the Word of God. No translation is infallible, and no man must pin his faith in the interpretation of a given phrase when he is uncertain what the Greek means. "But" it is objected, "this is all that our congregations have". Precisely: this is why ministers must have more. There is no atom of revealed truth which is useless: a lesser error may lead a soul into a greater error. If someone should send to a firm of publishers a commentary on a New Testament book and that firm was informed that the man knew no Greek they would send the manuscript back to author very quickly. But ministers are the commentator and expositor to their people. Often, our responsibility is to defend the truth against the onslaughts of error. The centre of our preaching is Jesus Christ and him crucified and one of the attacks of liberal theology today is that "propitiation" would better be translated "expiation" in the New Testament, the liberal finds the concept of the appeasing of the Father's wrath repugnant. It is not sufficient to meet assertions such as that with bold, contrary assertions, but with a knowledge of the *hilasmos* group of Greek words and their usage in Old and New Testaments to vindicate the historic understanding.

One of the qualifications for a teaching elder, Paul tells Timothy, is that he is "apt to teach" (1 Tim. 3:2), that is, that he has a didactic ability to teach the gospel correctly. Imagine an Ephesian farmer of the first century who is one of Timothy's elders. Consider his knowledge of the Greek language, its history, its religious movements, culture and the whole background against which the New Testament was written. To a preacher in distant Wales today all that is so much archaeological knowledge; a chasm of nineteen centuries must be crossed. However, after he has learned Greek and all the New Testament background he has simply attained to the level of an Ephesian farmer who was a teaching elder in the early church, and if he does not attain that level is he then "apt to teach"?

The history of the church is full of warnings of the dangers of ignorance of the Scriptures. The Church fathers had a pathetic knowledge of Greek; they could converse easily enough in Latin, for it was their mother tongue, but Augustine, for instance, had no knowledge of Hebrew and little knowledge of Greek and when he continued to translate *metanoia* by "penance" instead of "repentance" he was encouraging the growth of great error in the Church which the Reformation had to deal with.

It is sometimes argued that there have been men, much used of God, who were ignorant of the original languages. The truth is this, that the very best of these men have always lamented their dependence upon translations and have seen the vital necessity of getting into the original, men like Christmas Evans who, in his fortieth year and with the remembrance of much blessing behind him, gave himself no rest until he had acquired a thorough knowledge of both the biblical languages. However, one is somewhat relieved to read these words of Dabney, "It should be admitted that a critical knowledge of the Hebrew tongue is less essential to the pastor than of the Greek and its lack less blameable. For the New Testament resumes and restates all the doctrines of redemption contained in the Old Testament".[2]

What is the cultural climate today? Everywhere in the world there is a tremendous emphasis on education. It has a messianic significance; men are pinning their hopes of world redemption upon it. Students are no longer satisfied with an initial degree—"research," "post-graduate studies," these are status terms. All professions are insisting on their members studying and even we ourselves like to obtain the services of a well-read qualified man. If, for example, we are choosing a family doctor we appreciate being recommended one who attends medical conferences and hears top men, studies the best medical journals and keeps up with the latest advances in this field. All this could be vitally important; our child might have a rare condition and this knowledge of the proper treatment could be imperative for the whole future well-being of the child. On the other hand, ignorance could jeopardise a life. How much more we who are the physicians of men's souls should be untiring students of the word of God as it diagnoses man's condition and what is to be done to remedy that state.

2. The Consequences of Study

It cannot be questioned that all sermons would be wonderfully improved by greater diligence in preparation, especially by an earlier start in the week. Spurgeon once said, "If some men were sentenced to hear their own sermons they would soon cry out with Cain—My punishment is greater than I can bear!" A man may spend much time in study but achieve very little because he is ill-equipped just as a hewer of wood can spend two days labouring to attain his quota, whereas were he but to sharpen his axe the two days work could be done easily in one. "If the iron be blunt and he do not whet the edge then must he put forth more strength." If he loves his Master he will take time and grind the edge for an hour and he will find at the end of the day it was not time wasted and there will be a larger heap of wood cut.

What, then, are some of the consequences of study?

(a) *In evangelism.* Study equips us for evangelism because evangelism is persuasion, *i.e.* a reasonable presentation of the gospel, "Knowing therefore the terror of the Lord we persuade men": we marshall arguments to get them to change their minds. When Paul came to Thessalonica he went to the synagogue and "reasoned with them out of the scriptures, opening and alleging" the facts of the gospel to them (Acts 17:2, 3). In Corinth you find the same pattern, he "spake boldly for the space of three months, disputing and persuading the things concerning the kingdom of God" (Acts 19:8). Conversion is a response to the truth, believing, acknowledging and obeying it. The preaching of the gospel is always to the whole man and so never disregards man's mind. Of course, bare reasoning and persuading is insufficient, but it is not unnecessary. We argue with a sinner's mind and answer his intellectual problems *and* also we will plead with his heart so that his will might be moved. All the time we are trusting in the Holy Spirit. We will not present a partial Christ and ask for a partial response; we want the heart and the mind of the sinner to submit to Christ's Lordship; we want the whole man. Are ministers spending enough time in helping people's faith? Are we able to answer their problems if we do not even understand them? It seems to me that this has been the strength of Francis Schaeffer and the movement which he leads, that a number of intelligent young people with real problems resulting from the prevailing atheistic climate of education have found in him someone who compassionately listens and can give thoughtful answers to their questions. If the initial enthusiasm for Schaeffer brought an inevitable evangelical reaction of criticism, perhaps it is now time for a balanced assessment and to restore an appreciation of the place of attempting to understand contemporary attitudes towards Christianity to equip one to answer them.

(b) *In worship.* God is a Spirit and they that worship him must worship him in spirit, and also in truth. As Horatius Bonar says, "All wrong thoughts of God, whether of Father, Son or Spirit must cast a shadow over the soul that entertains them. In some cases the shadow may not be so deep and cold as in others; but never can it be a trifle. And it is this that furnishes the proper answer to the flippant question so often asked: Does it really matter what a man believes? All defective views of God's character tell upon the life of the soul and the peace of the conscience. We must think right thoughts of God if we would worship him as he desires to be worshipped, if we would live the life he wishes us to live, and enjoy the peace which he has provided for us."[3] One can also find Dr. Alexander Whyte testifying to the relation of right belief and the highest devotion when he writes, "One of the acknowledged masters of the spiritual life warns us against an unethical devotion. True spirituality, he insists, has always been orthodox. And the readers of the *Grammar of Assent* will remember with what masterly power and with what equal eloquence it is there set forth that the theology of the Creeds and Catechisms, when it is rightly understood and properly employed, appeals to the heart as much as to the head, to the imagination quite as much as to the understanding. And we cannot study Andrewes' book (his *Private*

Devotions), his closest confession of faith especially without discovering what a majesty, what a massiveness, what a depth and what a strength, as well as what an evangelical fervour and heartsomeness, his theology has given to his devotional life".[4]   Dr. J. H. Thornwell was greatly blessed on a certain occasion in reading the Westminster Confession, and Warfield also testifies to the same thing, writing, "we can ourselves testify from experience to the power of the Westminster Confession to quicken religious emotion, and to form and guide a deeply devotional life".[5]   There can be no question that, as Dr. Whyte writes, "all true theology is directly and richly and evangelically devotional".

Ministers often lament that their feelings are lagging far behind their knowledge and that this has resulted in an almost barren familiarity with sacred things.   This is only because it is the minister's greatest privilege to be thoroughly acquainted with the doctrines of the Word.   Other men, distracted by the pressures of life, and struggling for their existence, find it hard to get time to pause and consider God and his salvation.   This is the atmosphere of our life; it surrounds and encompasses us, and if all this should become commonplace to us then God forgive us; we are wearying of God!   Are we alive to our privileges?   Are we making full use of them?   Are we, by constant contact with divine things, growing in holiness, becoming every day more and more men of God?   If not then we are not maintaining the *status quo*: we are hardening.   Our studies are thus a most serious matter done for the Lord's sake and charged with the possibility of blessing, fitted to fill all our life with thoughts and feelings of God and his ways.   Cotton Mather wrote a little book on the training of the ministry which he entitled *Manductio Ad Ministerium* ("Guidance for the Ministry") but to which he added with a flash of illumination this sub-title, "The angels preparing to sound the trumpets".   This is an apt description of our studies.

(c) *In strengthening faith.*   The more we know of God's character, the greatness of his kingdom and the might of his power the more our faith in him should be deepened.   Who can study the Reformation period, or the doctrine of the person and work of the Holy Spirit without his appreciation of God's power being increased?   Dr. Lloyd-Jones writes, "the best thing a man can do when he feels that he knows all, and is elated and tempted to intellectual pride, is to pick up say the Journals of George Whitefield.   There he will read of how that man was used of God in England, Wales, Scotland and America, and also of his experiences of the love of Christ; and if he does not feel that he is but a worm, well then I suggest that he has never been regenerated.   We continually need to be humbled.   That is why balanced reading is an absolute essential".[6]   Paul prays for the Ephesian Christians that the eyes of their understanding be enlightened that they might *know* the greatness of God's power in the resurrection.   Why?   Because, Paul says, this power which God demonstrated in Christ's raising is *now available* to us who believe.   First of all

32

we must know in our minds the magnitude of God's power, then we will appropriate that power by faith alone. We study our God and discover that he is the God of Resurrection, the God of Revival and the God of Reformation and our faith is enlivened by this understanding.

(d) *In deepening love.* To know God is to love him. The more we understand of his character, his gospel, and his grace to that degree should our devotion be increased. So too, in the second great commandment, knowledge gained should increase our love for our neighbours. This is seen in the manner Paul addresses the Corinthian church. One problem in the fellowship was caused by certain of the weaker members who had a scrupulosity concerning eating meat which came from pagan temples and had been offered there to the idol. Others of the fellowship had a maturer faith; for them it was no problem eating such meat because they knew that idols had no power and that there was nothing contaminating in the meat. The extra knowledge of the truth which the strong men in the fellowship possessed resulted in their respecting the weaker brothers' scruples, thereby not forcing him to eat meat and go against his conscience and even occasionally doing without such meat themselves. Knowledge led them into freedom and into loving self-denial. What is the understanding of all mysteries and all knowledge without love? It is nothing. We are not only to be mighty in wielding the sword, but mighty in self-control when the sword is kept in its scabbard. Ministers of the gospel are to be characterised by a humble doing of the word. Thomas Manton likens disobedient Christians to children suffering from rickets: "Rickets cause great heads and weak feet. We are not only to dispute of the word, and talk of it, but to keep it. We must neither be all ear, nor all head, nor all tongue, but the feet must be exercised".[7]

These things are some of the benefits of study. Our libraries are not places of book-lined luxury, but a training camp where soldiers of Christ prepare for the warfare. There is little danger from too much preparation making us over-educated; the reverse is our problem. Of course great learning can be accompanied by a bad nature, but so too can a little learning. All we have learned multiplied by ten will not be too much for the work or more than the times demand. No matter how strong our zeal and spirit of devotion it will be no excuse for neglecting the discipline of study. Consider Spurgeon: who was more devout, more zealous and yet more devoted to learning or more profoundly anxious that study and religion should never be divorced? Hear again his famous exhortation on 2 Tim. 4:13, "Even an apostle must read. Some of our very ultra-Calvinistic brethren think that a minister who reads books and studies his sermon must be a very deplorable specimen of a preacher. A man who comes up into the pulpit, professes to take his text on the spot, and talks any quantity of nonsense, is the idol of many. If he will speak without premeditation, or pretend to do so, and never produce what they call a dish of dead men's brains—Oh! that is the preacher. How rebuked they are by the apostle!

33

c

He is inspired, and yet he wants books! He has been preaching at least for thirty years, and yet he wants books! He has seen the Lord, and yet he wants books! He had a wider experience than most men, and yet he wants books! He had been caught up into the third heaven, and heard things which it was unlawful for a man to utter, yet he wants books! He had written the major part of the New Testament, and yet he wants books! The apostle says to Timothy and so he says to every preacher, "Give thyself unto reading" (1 Tim. 4:13). . . . Renounce as much as you will all light literature, but study as much as possible sound theological works, especially the Puritanic writers, and expositions of the Bible. We are quite persuaded that the very best way for you to be spending your leisure, is to be either reading or praying. You may get much instruction from books which afterwards you may use as a true weapon in your Lord and Master's service. Paul cries, Bring the books!—join in the cry.

3. The Need for Discipline

Everyone has to discipline his life; this is the essence of the doctrine of vocation. The man called to be a roadsweeper cannot fulfil his duties by sweeping up a leaf here and a scrap of paper there as his fancy takes him, he has a schedule and daily duties to perform. The scientist involved in research does not wander into his laboratory and move from one piece of apparatus to another as a thought strikes him, progress comes through the most resolute application of ideas to scientific examination and scrutiny. Parents see how great is the need in their children of learning the blessings of being under authority, firstly of their parents and then, as they mature, of a self-imposed discipline.

How much, then, does a minister of the gospel with the comparative freedom of his schedule and absence of daily oversight, need to learn the essential nature of disciplined living. While not a few wage war for a smaller and smaller working week (thirty-five to forty hours) the average pastor works not less than seventy into which he must preach and visit, attend to correspondence, evangelism, counselling, writing, administration (which includes a busy telephone), not neglect his own family, deal with emergencies, give hospitality, maintain his own devotional life, pray, keep abreast with news and travel. The list is not full. It lacks a vital area without which it all lacks power. He must study!

What need he has for discipline! Consider the amount of books produced today; there is an absolute explosion of information and research. More than 30,000 religious titles are in print in Britain at the moment with 1,300 new titles appearing every year.

The rugged vitality of the modern Calvinistic movement has produced new publishers, authors, magazines and distributors. Who can keep abreast with all of this? There is the temptation to buy new books when they first appear and so never get round to reading the classics of the faith. Some books are worth reading ten times over while many new books are not worth the trouble of reading once. What is one to choose? What books are we to buy? Ministers' wives complain that their husbands have books on their shelves already which they have never read. It is true, but Baxter justifies this by saying, "a minister of the Gospel should have more books by him than he could read over, for particular uses, and to see the author's judgement occasionally, and to try other men's citations".

How important is the ministers' use of his time; for him there is special significance in the Psalmist's prayer, "So teach us to number our days that we may apply our hearts unto wisdom" (Ps. 90:12). We see the vast and edifying works of Baxter, Spurgeon, Luther and Owen and remember that they were all written in the midst of pressing pastoral duties, almost daily preaching engagements and with the most uncertain health. All of them had a deep sense of the value of time. Alleine declared, "Give me a Christian that counts his time more precious than gold". A contemporary prolific writer was Arthur Pink; all reports indicated he was a man of resolute and almost fanatical adherence to a study. Nothing could come between him and his labours. He is an example to us in all of this; we should hate an hour of idleness like an hour of vandalism.

The great need of the modern Reformed movement, is the simplification of the great truths of Calvinistic orthodoxy, that they become attractive and compelling to the average, evangelical church-goer. Our problem in rediscovering the breadth of biblical Christianity is rightly to popularise it and teach it to the people so that it lives for them too. A great need of the hour is the popular writing of orthodox themes so that what a man like William Barclay has done for Modernism could be done for the doctrines of grace. All the discipline of study is a striving for simplicity.

There are ancillary benefits from learning the discipline of study. All of our living is enriched, because our mental faculties are not isolated units in our personality. Church, family and all of society benefit from men who are disciplined in their life-styles. The minister who has learned this grace will be standing firm when a crisis arises in his congregation. He will not flap or panic, but will have been taught how to think and consider the ways of God; there is nothing new under the sun. What contradiction of professing believers did the apostle Paul endure against himself. He will be encouraged in the Word and calm his feelings in the discipline of its study.

Failure to discipline one's ministry will show itself in many ways. The undisciplined minister is always complaining that he has "no time to read". He does read the evangelical magazines and his own denominational paper; he reads paperbacks and neglects the classic works (though they may well be on his shelves). He reads the New Testament but is ignorant of the Old Testament. He knows something of the history of his own denomination, though this is a vestige of his student days. Church history for him starts with the Reformation and he specialises, he believes, in missionary biography and revivals. He has probably built up quite a library of books on the occult, witchcraft, exorcism and demon-possession and here he may consider himself an "authority". Such are some of the tell-tale clues of an undisciplined minister's reading.

Such men cannot stand on the slippery floor of a popular pulpit for long. They may have a transient popularity and be of some little usefulness without deeper study, but it is all a fire of straw that soon burns out. Soon they are on the move to other pulpits. The preacher who is called upon to be constantly pouring out and seldom pouring in can pour out for just so long. The great evil of most sermons is lack of content and the antidote is perpetual acquaintance with God-honouring literature. Yet this alone is insufficient. Truth is impersonal; the God of truth must be regularly consulted. The Author of the Bible and the Illuminator of holy writers must actually be addressed in entreaties and petitions.

4. The Means of Discipline

The principal means of attaining discipline in study are spiritual, because self-control is a fruit of the spirit. It is a grace which the Christian must add to knowledge (2 Peter 1:6), which will make him neither barren nor unfruitful in the knowledge of our Lord Jesus Christ. The attainment of self-control is one of the evidences of the certainty of his calling and election. This is no option for God's servant but something to be sought for earnestly. It is a characteristic of the Christian soldier that he is a man under discipline, the work in which he is engaged is arduous, calling for the exertion of all his powers. He has many enemies to overcome within and without. Within are sloth, lack of faith, despondency, love of ease, desire for fame, love of money and power and a spirit of langour. Without are error, disregard of the truth, ignorance, vice in all its forms, infidelity. How he must cry daily for the grace of self-control to be poured out upon him! His whole time and strength are not sufficient for the work. He dare not entangle himself with the affairs of this world—unnecessary secular employment, literary or political pursuits, and even general enterprises of benevolence are not to distract his interest and eat up his time. Rather, he must see the great goal of his calling as the ministry of the Word and prayer and to that end must display the qualities of endurance, patience and indomitable perseverance.

To have these highest aims before him is the indispensable means of attaining self-discipline, without which all the equipment of a minister's office and study is worse than useless. Another means of attaining self-discipline is negative; he must lay to his conscience the sin of an ill-disciplined life. He must recall that Sunday service when a contact visited the church for the first time and the sermon had been hastily put together lacking in structure, content and application. The man's interest was not aroused and his conscience was untouched. Politely

thankful at the door he did not return. The trumpet had given an uncertain sound. How many times have there been occasions such as that?
McCheyne says, "I would rather beg my bread, than preach without
success". Is our failure in part due to such poor preparation? Hear
again the admonition of Richard Baxter: "If we were duly devoted to our
work, we would not be so negligent in our studies. Few men are at the
pains that are necessary for the right informing of their understandings,
and fitting them for their further work. Some men have no delight in
their studies, but take only now and then an hour, as an unwelcome task
which they are forced to fulfil, and are glad when they are from under the
yoke. Will neither the natural desire of knowledge, nor the consciousness
of our great ignorance and weakness, nor the sense of the weight of our
ministerial work—will none of all these things keep us closer to our studies
and make us more diligent in seeking after the truth? O what abundance
of things are there that a minister should understand! And what a great
defect is it to be ignorant of them! And how much shall we miss such
knowledge in our work! Many ministers study only to compose their
sermons, and very little more, when there are so many books to be read,
and so many matters that we should not be unacquainted with. Nay, in
the study of our sermons we are too negligent, gathering only a few naked
truths, and not considering of the most forcible expressions by which we
may set them home to men's consciences and hearts. We must study how
to convince and get within men, and how to bring each truth to the quick,
and not leave all this to our extemporary promptitude, unless in cases of
necessity. Certainly, brethren, experience will teach you, that men are
not made learned or wise without hard study, and unwearied labour and
experience. If we were duly devoted to our work, it would be done more
vigorously, and more seriously, than it is by most of us. How few
ministers do preach with all their might. . . Oh, brethren, how plainly,
how closely, how earnestly, should we deliver a message of such importance as ours, when the everlasting life or everlasting death of our fellow-
men is involved in it!. . . In the name of God, brethren, labour to awaken
your own hearts, before you go to the pulpit, that you may be fit to awaken
the hearts of sinners".[8]

Thus, we are reminded so stirringly that discipline is to be sought and
maintained as a gift of God by much prayer, which itself is motivated by
compassion for our hearers, and an appreciation of the absolute indispen-
sability of this grace.

Yet one does not despise practical exhortations as to the strengthening
of this grace, these too are means God blesses to our usefulness. Chiefly,
the need of a schedule cannot be overemphasised. With few hours to
do so much, the danger of frittering away our time in one or another
interest is very great. A year's wall-chart with a space for every day is
useful in seeing the over-all pattern of the months ahead. It will indicate
the most suitable periods for larger projects. Also weekly and daily

priority sheets help to structure visiting, letter-writing, sermon-preparation and study all to some considerable advantage. Yet another practical means of studying is the adoption by a group of ministers in an area of a number of Christian classics which they plan to read within a year, meeting occasionally to read parts together and comment and discuss the benefits and application of the book to their own situations. Some of the men who have helped me in the church have met with me to read alternate paragraphs of books such as Bridges' *The Christian Ministry* and D. M. M. Mc'Intyre's *Hidden Life of Prayer*. Of course, in all such schemes and schedules *flexibility* should be the chief characteristic, so that various emergencies can be handled. Also, there must be regard for one's own habits and abilities; some men study better in blocks of time and others in a period at this time and then an hour at that time. Having a room as a study is generally recognised to be most advantageous, as it conditions a man to work in familiar surroundings with established associations of mental activity. Having enough working surface is as important an item as anything else in the study so that correspondence, articles, sermons, etc. do not all have to be moved away when there is a change in labours. Certain men profit from studying in a library or reading-room; this should be encouraged. Home comforts, lengthy coffee-breaks and romping with the children are all out of temptation's way! However, one remembers how Charles Hodge had the handles on his study door put especially low so that his children could come in and talk to him any time they wanted to, and that fatherly love showed itself in three generations of professors of systematic theology at Princeton. Other men would profit from a sabbatical when they could return to college for extra, specialised study under supervision. Such organisations as the Open University offer courses of study on the Reformation period for ministers, although the lecturers would not be especially sympathetic to the conservative interpretation of that period. Yet, even without any supervision it is possible for the minister to make great progress in biblical languages and background. The Rev. E. W. Johnson is the minister of Calvary Baptist Church, Pine Bluff, Arkansas and the author of the stimulating *Sovereign Grace Message*. In the November 1973 issue he wrote of training men for the ministry and of his own habits of study: "I have had young preachers come to me and ask about their moving to Pine Bluff and studying the Bible under my guidance. I have told them that if they did this, I would recommend that they study the Bible as I have done over the years. My method has been to learn how to read Greek and Hebrew and then make my own commentary of the Bible, translating the Greek and the Hebrew and accumulating notes of the texts. These commentaries which I have formed are of no value to anyone. Their value to me was in the making of them. In recent years, in addition to carefully translating the Hebrew or the Greek texts of the Bible, I read the passage under review in two ancient versions, and in three modern versions. I read the Old Testament passage in that ancient version known as the Septuagint, and both the

Old Testament and New Testament passages in that ancient version known as the Vulgate, Jerome's Latin Bible. The modern translations in which I read the passages under study are Martin Luther's German, made about 1522, de Reina's Spanish version, first made in 1569 by Casiodoro de Reina and revised in 1602 by Cipriano de Valera, a most excellent translation, and, of course, our own King James Version, made in 1611. I do not have any thorough knowledge of either the Latin, the German or the Spanish, but have enough familiarity with them to be able to read the Bible. Language is a *learn by doing* proposition, and the trick in any *learn by doing* discipline is to do something you enjoy doing and is profitable while you are learning by doing. In my Bible study I have simply learned how to pronounce these languages, gained some understanding of their grammar, accumulated a small vocabulary, and then started reading the Bible".

This example is quoted as an encouragement to spread our wings and fly to new areas of study from which, hitherto, we had timorously shrunk. The freedom we have is not licence to do what we like but privilege to do what we must. This freedom is hardly won and must be zealously guarded. God grant that we may all know the blessings of the discipline of study.

The following sources are recommended for further reading:

Selected Shorter Writings of Benjamin B. Warfield, Volumes I and II. Volume I "Our Seminary Curriculum" (pp. 369-373), "The Purpose of the Seminary" (pp. 374-378) and especially "The Religious Life of Theological Students" (pp. 411-428), which article has subsequently appeared as a separate pamphlet and merits the attention of all theological students. Then in Volume II there is the equally important paper on "Spiritual Culture in the Theological Seminary" (pp. 468-497). Again, *Your Mind Matters*, subtitled "The Place of the Mind in the Christian Life", by John Stott is one of the best things he has written and puts us in his debt. *The Christian Ministry* by Charles Bridges is profitable on all aspects of the ministry, and his section on "Habits of General Study" (pp. 33-49) is helpful. More recently Dr. Martyn Lloyd-Jones has lightened us in our understanding of "the highest and the greatest and the most glorious calling to which anyone can ever be called" in *Preaching and Preachers* and the chapters entitled "The Preparation of the Preacher" and "The Preparation of the Sermon" (pp. 165-205) are particularly useful. Finally, one recommends unhesitatingly some notes from Dr. J. W. Alexander's Letters to Young Ministers entitled "Ministerial Study" which appeared in the *Banner of Truth Magazine* No. 8, August 1957.

References——

[1] *Selected Shorter Writings*, Vol. I, "The Purpose of the Seminary," p. 378. [2] *Discussions Evangelical and Theological*, Vol. II, "A Thoroughly Educated Ministry," pp. 651-677. [3] *The Gospel of the Spirit's Love* p. 22. [4] *Lancelot Andrewes and His Private Devotions*, pp. 49-51. [5] *Selected Shorter Writings*, Vol. II, p. 286. [6] *Preaching and Preachers*, p. 179. [7] *Exposition of John 17*, p. 117. [8] *Reformed Pastor*, Ch. III, "Application," II, 1, "By Negligent Studies".

The
Local Church
and Evangelism

Erroll Hulse

THESE ARE DAYS IN WHICH THERE IS GREAT STRESS ON ORGANIZATION, including the organization of great world congresses to talk about evangelism. What are we to think of these huge affairs? Where does the local church figure in evangelism? What is evangelism? Does theology have anything to do with evangelism? And what about the relationship of preaching to evangelism? These are some of the issues which I wish to address in the following article. To begin with an issue might be discussed which is highly relevant and which affects most local churches. I refer to evangelistic organizations outside the churches. Let us look at an example.

An article in Crusade magazine, November 1973, is devoted to a description of a new evangelistic project. Conscious of the fact that this new organised effort, nicknamed *Power*, is not the first scheme to descend on the churches from an organisation outside the churches, the writer declares: "Whilst it is true that *Power* cannot be described as a truly 'grass roots' movement (can anything?), it is doubtful if any project has been the subject of such widespread and intensive discussion at all levels as this one."

Several comments are called for. The project, it is claimed, is the subject of "widespread and intensive discussion". This generation has talked more about evangelism than any other, with massive amounts of money being spent on yet more discussion. World Congresses on evangelism and about evangelization have multiplied words about this subject. Yet talking about evangelism has not arrested spiritual declension going on around us. Furthermore, modern evangelism, particularly as practised in America, has not arrested the awful moral decline and darkness of the world whereas the teaching ministry exercised in times of reformation has dispelled darkness and brought light to the nations.

Turning to the Crusade article again the comment about "grass roots" needs analysis. "*Power* cannot be described as a truly 'grass roots' movement (can anything?)", says the writer. In reply I would assert the claim that Christians of previous generations did indeed *practise* "grass roots" evangelism, rather than merely talking about it. They practised it spontaneously because their roots were in theology. They drew their spiritual life from the Word and hence evangelism was a way of life, rather than a technique to be learned. They could do no other than witness to the Lord Jesus Christ and teach his salvation to others.

The roots of evangelism are embedded in the local church which derives its life from Christ, as he is set forth in the whole of Scripture. The members evangelise as they are nourished by the preaching, strengthened by the corporate prayer and worship of the church and encouraged by fellowship. Christians who abide in Christ by abiding in a true local church will evangelise spontaneously. They can do no other. If the churches are not producing evangelism in this spontaneous way, the way to recovery is not by the imposition of organised efforts upon the churches from without. The only way is by reformation and revival taking place within. The new organisation called *Power*, like all its predecessors, is superficial for it ignores the urgent need for reformation and revival *in* the churches. Moreover having attended the Berlin World Congress for Evangelism and spent time analysing its effects and writing an appraisal of it, I feel very strongly that such Congresses do more harm than good. Not only is ecumenical evangelism promoted, but Arminian teaching and apologetics are encouraged. The overall tendency is for churches to continue to depend on extramural efforts, *i.e.* efforts coming in from the outside. We should rather devote our time and energy to "grass roots" evangelism, evangelism that springs up all the year round—not just an annual effort, but outreach from healthy, scripturally governed churches. I propose to deal with the subject in the following way:

1. *Evangelism defined from the New Testament in which we also see what evangelism is not.*
2. *A dynamic theology is the foundation of evangelism.*
3. *A dynamic Church is the agent of evangelism.*
4. *Dynamic preaching the chief instrument of the Church's evangelism.*

5. *A dynamic communication of the Gospel to every creature springs from local churches.*

1. Evangelism defined from the New Testament in which we also see what evangelism is not.

Evangelism is the preaching of the Gospel to every creature. There is no limit. We are to go into all the world. No kind of person is excepted, old or young, male or female, rich or poor, weak or strong. There is a priority. The Gospel is to be preached to the Jew first (Rom. 1:16). Apart from the application to the Hebrew people there is another lesson to be drawn from this priority. The Gospel must be preached and applied to our own immediate family circle first. The Christian mother teaching the Gospel to her children is a power that has worked to the salvation of multitudes. Some of the best missionaries have emerged from Christian homes, men such as John C. Paton and William Burns.

When we define evangelism we include comprehensiveness as well as contact. To have a five minute chat about the Gospel with every creature in the world is not to evangelize the world. That is contact alone. That is an introduction and such is valuable indeed, but evangelism is much more than that. Evangelism is comprehensive. Our Lord states this comprehensiveness as follows: "Go ye therefore, and teach all nations, baptizing them in the name of the Father, and of the Son, and of the Holy Ghost: Teaching them to observe all things whatsoever I have commanded you" (Matt. 28:19). The teaching is to be such that those disciples or learners that are made are prepared for baptism into the Trinity and such baptism presupposes a thorough and detailed understanding of each of the three persons of the Trinity. Think of the colossal ignorance, the woeful darkness, the terrible deception about Creation, the Bible, God, Christ, and the Church prevalent today. The task of dispelling this ignorance and deception by way of proclamation and teaching is enormous. Until the end of the world we are to tackle this task with intelligence, courage, energy and dependence upon the Lord who is with us to the end of the age.

Evangelism, then, is the preaching of the Gospel in detail and in a thorough manner to every creature. If people will have nothing to do with it we do not give up but persevere in the knowledge that this is what our Lord has commanded and therefore in wholehearted obedience we will continue.

Having given this brief definition we can now observe what evangelism is not.

(i) *Evangelism is not John 3:16 in isolation*

We must not think that if we shout out a few texts on a street corner we have fulfilled our evangelistic responsibilities. Favourable sites for open air preaching in this modern world of heavy traffic noise are rare and should be utilized wherever there is reasonable prospect of a listening audience. But if such is secured and used regularly it forms only one means of

42

evangelism. Likewise when literature is distributed we must remember that our dropping a few printed tracts or leaflets through letter boxes, while better than nothing, falls far short of the great commission to evangelize. Much that is done today can be likened to a farmer who, instead of engaging in the systematic labour of ploughing and planting ten acres of corn, goes out for five minutes and throws a few handfuls of seed on the ground, the most of which is immediately devoured by the birds of the air.

(ii) *Evangelism is not revival*

Recently I procured a cassette tape on the subject of evangelism by a well known preacher. I played it several times and was edified by it but in actual fact he did not say a word about evangelism! It was all about revival and the theology of revival. I believe in revival with all my heart, but revival is not evangelism. Revival will lead to better and more effective evangelism. If, however, we slip into thinking that we can do nothing until revival comes—and it has not come now for well over a century—then we slip into irresponsibility of the most diabolical kind. Our Lord commanded evangelism. We are to obey as best we can. We may be weak and the churches may be weak. Nevertheless we may never excuse ourselves. Evangelism is an abiding obligation to the end of the age. Our Lord did not say that we ought only to evangelize when he sends revival. The principle of Psalm 126 is apposite here. If we sow in tears we shall reap in joy. We are not to excuse our sloth by saying to ourselves, "An well, in revival hundreds will be saved, but all our efforts bear little fruit—but one here and two there—so I am going to ease up and wait for revival!" Revival may never be seen in this generation yet multitudes will continue to be saved one by one throughout all nations, through the ordinary outreach and witness of local churches.

(iii) *Evangelism is not the establishment of a preaching centre*

Some dear brothers in the ministry that I know think that all they need do for evangelism is preach in a pulpit three times a week. They pray for people to come in but such prayer shows a lack of common sense for the people round about do not even know of the existence of that pulpit. God uses means. He will not send angels to tell the people. *We* must tell the people and if they are utterly opposed to going to a church then we must resort to other means of teaching them. Our Lord did not lay it down as a condition that the teaching must begin in ecclesiastical buildings. It becomes clear to disciples that Christ and his people are one and that there are decided obligations to make use of the means of grace and to gather where God's people gather. Initially, however, we must be ready to teach people in homes, either theirs or ours.

The pulpit, as we shall see, is the Church's most powerful instrument in the conversion of souls but we must never imagine that the mandate to evangelize is fulfilled merely by the establishment and maintenance of a preaching centre.

(iv) *Evangelism is not a special crusade or campaign*

The idea has long prevailed in evangelical churches that for the most part evangelism consists of a special evangelistic effort once or twice a year, in which an evangelist is employed for a week or two. At the end of every meeting a call is made for decisions for Christ. At the end of the campaign the results are made known. Some souls may have been drawn in and truly saved by this method and in some cases churches have been quickened to recognize their responsibilities. Having come from this kind of tradition and having observed this practice in various places I have noticed that very little, if any, regular, consistent evangelism is carried on in these churches. The tendency is to make a big effort for the special campaign and then to go back to doing nothing until the next effort comes along. In addition to this, the system is fraudulent and dishonest in the extreme—it is a big lie! Only a small fraction of those advertised as though they were converts continue. When the truth is exposed the excuse is made: "it was worth it for one or two!" It is disgraceful that dishonesty of this kind should be practised by some platform evangelists who have to advertise their success in order to continue in business. If all the decisions that have been reported in such a way as to give the idea that they were converts were in fact true converts, we would be living in the millennium by now! Lying at the root of it all is defective theology which brings us to consider the question of doctrine upon which the apostles, particularly Paul, laid such stress.

2. A dynamic theology is the foundation of evangelism

Our age is an age of power, an age in which people look for and admire the dynamic. Men talk constantly about power: military power, political power, industrial power, economic power. Our Lord in sending his disciples out to evangelize the world, declared that all power belonged to him. He alone has the power to regenerate and quicken sinners. He alone has the dynamic to create new life. A theology that does not come to grips with the sovereign power of God is less than dynamic. "All power is given to me—go ye therefore." Our knowledge of God (theology) and the fact that Christ is now making application of the redemption he has secured for his people forms the foundation of evangelism, the basis upon which we proceed to the work. The knowledge that our Lord has power to quicken whom he wills invests our persevering efforts with hope and expectancy. The doctrine of election, far from shutting out sinners, is the reason for their being gathered in. As we evangelize we soon discover that "there is none that seeketh after God" (Rom. 3:11). But we are encouraged by the sovereignty of God and such statements as, "All things are delivered unto me of my Father: and no man knoweth the

44

Son, but the Father; neither knoweth any man the Father, save the Son, and he to whomsoever the Son will reveal him" (Matt. 11:27).

Theology is a knowledge of God. We are to teach all truth, particularly those truths which pertain to the knowledge of the Father, the Son and the Holy Ghost into whom the converts are baptized. What makes theology dynamic? The Holy Spirit, for he comes like the wind to regenerate and quicken. To us the proclamation belongs. To the Spirit regeneration belongs. We are to command men to repent and to believe. We are to exhort, urge, plead, expound and teach. We can do all this. But we cannot regenerate. "Of his own will begot he us with the word of truth" (James 1:18).

Regeneration precedes faith and repentance. Repentance is God's gift (Acts 5:31 and 11:18). Likewise faith is God's gift to all his elect people. It is not man's faith which causes election but election which causes man's faith. (If the reader is in doubt about this a study of the following Scriptures will be helpful: Deut. 7:7, 8, Hos. 14:4, John 6:37, 39, 44, 12:32, 1 Cor. 1:27, 28, Eph. 2:8, 9, 2 Pet. 1:1, 1 John 4:10, 19). This is the hinge upon which the whole issue turns. Modern evangelism is based on the notion that the preacher must preach to obtain man's response in order that God might then regenerate. Human response can be obtained by the exertion of pressure. By means of a call for decisions a visible result can be obtained. Our interest is in regeneration. When souls are quickened they soon make their presence felt as they did under Peter's preaching: "Men and brethren, what shall we do?" (Acts 2:37). Those who follow in the apostolic tradition preach for regeneration. They are not interested in a harvest of hay, wood and stubble. They look for gold, silver and precious stones.[1]

Preaching which is vindicated by the living, dynamic, almighty regeneration of God in which souls are brought to life is magnificent. In contrast to this, evangelism in which teaching and doctrine are minimized, and man-centred religion predominates, with the emphasis on entertainment, is weak and disappointing, because those who profess to have made decisions soon fall away.

The question of the centrality of theology was avoided at the World Congress on Evangelism at Berlin in 1966. The outcome was summarized as follows:
"In contrast with the results of other historic assemblies the Congress papers will reflect the theological weakness and uncertainty which characterizes twentieth century evangelicalism. Blessings and curses are mingled together. The atmosphere is grey. The pure air of the Gospel is there, but so is the smog. The sun does shine, but dimly through the smoke and fumes of compromise and doctrinal confusion.

"The Christian Church today faces one of the greatest crises of all time. In past centuries some truths have been assailed. Now the very foundations of the faith are being rejected.   The World Congress on Evangelism revealed how ill-equipped evangelicals are to face this crisis.   Inarticulate in doctrine and man-centred in outlook, many evangelical leaders are unable even to define what the historic faith is, let alone teach it.   The result is that a diluted theology within the churches has produced a shallow and ignorant generation of Christians."[2]

The World Congress on Evangelization at Lausanne in 1974 proceeded on the basis that theological issues had been clarified at Berlin.   Lausanne was even more confused theologically than Berlin.

It is commonly understood that a heresy is something which destroys the Gospel whereas an error is that which is wrong and misleading but which is not serious enough to destroy the Gospel.   Two heresies in particular destroy the Gospel as far as its evangelistic thrust is concerned.   One is hyper-Calvinism in which the free offers of the Gospel are denied and in which an excuse is made of the fact that men are dead in sin and therefore there is no point in evangelizing.   Total human responsibility (men know that they ought to repent and believe the Gospel) must be maintained together with faith in the sovereignty of God.   These matters cannot be reconciled to human logic.   The hyper-Calvinist in his desire to be logical comes to the wrong conclusion that it is inconsistent to command sinners to repent and believe when they are unable to do so, which is entirely an unbiblical and false conclusion!

The other heresy which destroys true evangelism is decisionism.   This system also follows human logic.   If God commands sinners to repent and believe, then obviously, reason the decisionists, they must be able to do so.   Therefore, without any further ado, we employ every device at our disposal to get men to make a decision.   Clive Tyler of Cape Town, in his enlightening article, demonstrates the harmful practices which Finney's logic has led to in the churches.[3]   That which stops short of God's regeneration deceives souls into a false assurance and creates havoc in the churches because of the addition of false converts.   Paul preached repentance toward God and faith in the Lord Jesus Christ (Acts 20:21).   God commands all men everywhere to repent (Acts 17:30).   To us belongs the proclamation to every creature.   To God belongs the increase.

3.   A dynamic Church is the agent of evangelism

The nature of the Church

That the Church is the agent of evangelism can be seen, firstly, by observing the nature of the Church and, secondly, by examining the example of the Church in the New Testament.   Our Lord commissioned his disciples to go and, "teach all nations, baptizing them in the name of the Father, and of the Son, and of the Holy Ghost" (Matt. 28:19).   Those so baptized are joined to the body of Christ which is the Church.   The Church is described by different analogies. The predominant analogy is that of the human body. Each member of the Church has a function. (Rom. 12:4, the word "office" is better translated *function* from the Greek word *prazin*; 1 Cor. 12:12-27; Eph. 4:16.) Union with Christ by faith is essential in order to be a member of Christ's Church. To be joined to Christ is to live or to have spiritual life. The living union is illustrated by the analogy of the vine and the branches (John 15:1-11). Christ's body, or Church, is like the vine. To abide in it is to have life but to be severed from it is to be severed from the means of grace given by Christ to his Church which leads to drying up and ultimately to spiritual death. A further analogy is that used by Paul in Ephesians where he likens the Church to a living building. It is organic, for it is growing. The Holy Spirit dwells in this building in which all the members are like living stones, fitly framed together in harmony, union and common purpose. (See also 1 Pet. 2:5.)

Essential to the Church is the purity of her membership. The stones must be living for they are to offer up spiritual sacrifices. That they must be living is further seen in that they are to grow and increase in love (Eph. 4:16). It is self-evident that nothing will contribute more quickly to the destruction of the Church than the entrance into her visible membership of those who are hostile to her doctrines and to her Head. Christ has, however, made provision for the purity of the Church to be maintained by means of discipline. This discipline was vested first in the apostles for the establishment of the New Testament Church and following that extraordinary period of establishment this discipline is vested in elders. Stress has been laid on the fact that the Church is a living body, this life being well illustrated by the human body, the vine and the living building. This life is exclusive. It belongs to the Church alone. Therefore evangelism emanates from the life of the Church for the enlargement of none other than the Church. Furthermore, the body of truth upon which evangelism is based is entrusted to the Church which is "the pillar and ground of the truth" (1 Tim. 3:15). The truth, together with the authority to propagate, defend and maintain it, is vested in the Church alone and the Church alone is commissioned to evangelize by taking the teaching to all nations, and by preaching the Gospel to every creature. The converts or disciples that are made are added to the parent body by baptism and each one is subject to the discipline of the elders of that body.

The Example of the New Testament Church

This principle is illustrated throughout the book of Acts. All the evangelism issued or came from the Church. All the converts made were baptized into the Church. "Repent and be baptized every one of you," declares Peter (Acts 2:38). When Paul writes to the Corinthians he writes to the Church at Corinth, the composition of which he specifies exactly as "them that are sanctified in Christ Jesus, called to be saints".

To them he writes and no other. Paul insists that discipline be maintained to preserve the purity of the body or the membership at Corinth (1 Cor. 5), just as Peter was used to maintain the purity of the Church at Jerusalem by the removal of Ananias and Sapphira (Acts 5).

Every true local church is an expression in an area of the body of Christ. The life of Christ is seen in that body as it can be seen in no other group of people on earth. The members of that local church are joined to Christ. They have his life and to have his life is to have dynamic life. The Holy Spirit dwells in and fills the members of the local church. Such love of people for each other the world has never seen. This is no small factor in convincing them that the Gospel is true (John 17:21). Such unity and such affection for God and devotedness in worship as expressed in the local church the world has never witnessed. The members of Christ's body found in the local church should have no peers when it comes to hospitality and good works. The inhabitants round about observe in them a people who suffer with meekness, who rejoice in God's goodness, whose lives are blameless and who abound in the truth which has brought transformation and eternal life to them. Thus the dynamic local church is God's agent for evangelism. The whole local church is involved. All members evangelize by life and lip and support some of their number who have been recognized and set apart, not only for the oversight and the maintenance of discipline, but for the public preaching of the Word. Care is taken to fulfil the high standards of correct doctrine insisted upon by the Scriptures (Acts 20:27-32; 1 Tim. 4:16; Titus 1:9 and 2:1). Those recognized in this way lead the flock in evangelism. The work is a corporate work and the elders or leaders do not act independently but see every member as having some part to play.

In the New Testament we see all the preaching coming from the Church as expressed in the local churches whether at Antioch, Corinth, Ephesus or elsewhere. All converts were added to the churches. All preachers were subject to the discipline of the churches and, if travelling abroad, were sent out by one church or another. Even the great apostle Paul did not go unsent or independently. He and Barnabas, after prayer and fasting, were sent out by the church at Antioch and to that church they returned and reported after their journeys.

Wrong practice in evangelism today

Independent evangelists, some of whom set up their own evangelistic organizations, are popular today. Some churches which are far from dynamic and which have poor preaching; little, if any, discipline; badly attended prayer meetings and a poor reputation in the towns where they are found, often resort to evangelistic campaigns to give them a boost. There is a flurry of activity and for a time a special effort is made to reach out to the neighbourhood. Contacts are made and there may be some

48

additions to the church. After the excitement of the special effort all the unsolved problems emerge once more—the lack of doctrine, the lack of oversight and discipline and the lack of consistent week by week outreach. The real problems are not solved by an evangelistic campaign. Evangelism does not produce life in the church. Rather, life in the church produces evangelism. Consistent, all-the-year-round evangelism will emerge when the churches are reformed and when due heed is given to the order which God has ordained by way of Scriptural church government, teaching and pastoral oversight. When such reformation takes place by the power of the Holy Spirit and He surges through or empowers the Scriptural order God has specified in his Word, evangelism will be irresistible and spontaneous. The people will not need to be bullied into it. Nobody will be able to stop them doing it!

Evangelistic societies which operate independently of the churches reason that they are needed because the churches are lifeless and dead. The churches, they argue, do not evangelize. Therefore, they contend, it is necessary to have evangelistic organizations to do the work. Yet these organizations appeal for money and depend on the churches for their existence. The evangelists are not subject to the authority of the churches. Their abilities, energies and resources are not channelled into churches but into separate organizations. Their lives, their thoughts and their practice are not moulded by the realities of local church life. They are responsible for their doctrine, their practice, and their methods to no one but themselves. That the forms of entertainment and the gimmicks they use to gain an audience are harmful to the true worship of God does not concern them. They do not have to face basic issues at local church level. They are independent of the churches and can act as they please.

When evangelistic organizations become huge in power and influence their own interests are predominant and they become a curse to the churches. There may be great talk about evangelizing the world by the end of the twentieth century, but in fact an enormous sum of money and time is spent merely on promoting a colossal organization and the system of evangelistic societies as a whole. In order to bolster up and support the needs of the evangelistic societies two matters are essential. One is the maintenance of Arminian or decisionist doctrine and the other is the promotion of Ecumenical evangelism. Should anyone preach free grace doctrine at a world Congress for Evangelism it will not make any impact for the simple reason that such convictions represent but one viewpoint among many. Synergism is the order of the day at these Congresses. Synergism is the combination of Arminian and Calvinistic concepts—the blending of truth with error. You take the five points of Calvinism, say on your right hand, and the five points of Arminianism on your left, you fold your two hands and ten fingers together and, hey presto!—perfect truth is the result! Even the apostle Paul would be baffled by one of these Congresses of Evangelism! His voice would simply be drowned by a

49

hundred others—huge mountains of words and papers—and the end result? —Arminianism and Ecumenism! I can well imagine Paul's astonishment to observe the truth he made clear buried under such an enormous pile of words and papers!

Let us consider Ecumenism and its implications at the local level. Ministers of true local churches are labouring to fulfil the command of Christ to teach, preach, administer baptism and the Lord's supper, maintain discipline and evangelize. In most cases they battle and struggle with the problem of Modernistic churches in which false ministers (wolves in sheep's clothing) deny the faith by rejecting the authority of Scripture and such basic truths as the wrath of God, the Judgment, hell, the atonement, the deity of Christ and the necessity of the New Birth. In some parts evangelical ministers are opposed by Roman Catholic, Anglo Catholic and Modernist ministers all working together in the Ecumenical movement. Along comes the Evangelistic Crusade which, in order to have adequate support, co-operates with all these alien bodies. When evangelical ministers are not prepared to join in and unite with such an effort they are accused of narrow-mindedness and disinterest in the great work of evangelism.

Not only independent evangelistic societies but all societies must be subject to the local churches. In no other place is spiritual authority vested but the local church. To no other place are disciples ingathered, taught and incorporated (Eph. 4:16). The Church, as represented by spiritual local churches throughout the world, is alone the object of Christ's saving love (Acts 20:28). It is high time that we thought in terms of dynamic churches alone as God's agent for evangelism!

4. Dynamic preaching the chief instrument of the Church's evangelism

It is not by the wisdom of men that souls are saved, but by the foolishness of preaching (1 Cor. 1:21). Through the ministry of the pulpit believers are fed and by means of the *same* ministry converts are made. Since so much depends on powerful and edifying preaching how careful ought we to be to safeguard the pulpit. If the flock is to be fed, then the preaching needs to be expository, systematic and doctrinal. Happily, such a ministry is well suited to evangelism for all parts of Scripture, including the doctrine of election, can be applied to unbelievers. Election implies total depravity. Since all men have rejected God he is free to save whom he wills. If he saves an enemy then that is an act of grace. I maintain that any part of Scripture can be preached evangelistically. We are to teach all things— all truth we find in Scripture. Thus teaching should be powerful, convicting, inspiring and relevant.

With regard to the evangelistic aspect of the pulpit ministry, I would suggest five factors of which the preacher should always be mindful.

(i) *Biblical content.* God should be set forth in his attributes. Who is God? God is Creator, God is holy, God is just, God will judge all men.

Content is essential in the preaching, but this content should be arresting, it should be interesting, it should be relevant and delivered in a powerful manner. There should be content always. That we are living in an age of education for all highlights this requirement. This is an age of education, far more so than in previous generations. Content and substance in the preaching does not in itself convert. What I am trying to explain is the fact that most people are repulsed from a natural point of view by mere emotionalism. They can recognize when there is real content and substance to what is said. It is interesting to observe how surprised people are to discover far more than they ever imagined. They just thought we were governed by emotions alone but then they discover we are a thinking people, that we are concerned about the application of the Gospel to every aspect of life. They may argue and disagree yet they are drawn back again and again and find themselves arrested and convicted by the truth of God.

(ii) *The moral law.* The Gospel is for sinners only, so our first task is to convince people that they are sinners. They are totally depraved, vile, evil, wicked sinners. These words sound extreme but when the full meaning of transgression against a holy God is realised by means of the law, they are no longer extreme words but true words. In exposition of the moral law there ought to be variety, directness and personal application. I have found Thomas Watson's book a help in understanding the Ten Commandments. The Larger Catechism is a great help, for it explains in precise terms the different ways in which the law is broken. Are we preaching the moral law? Is the Holy Spirit convincing sinners by the law through our preaching?

(iii) *Justification by free grace.* I believe we should always be conscious of the wonder of God's grace when we preach. God in his mercy comes to save all kinds of sinners. This is the wonder of grace. He freely justifies the sinner who believes. No matter how bad a man has been, no matter how foul he is, God can save him and give him a free justification —instantaneously and once and for all. This is why we give glory to God for the wonder of his grace. Everything is to this end: "the praise of the glory of God's grace" (Eph. 1:6). When sinners are saved that grace is magnified. Therefore we expect that sinners will be saved.

(iv) *The free offers of the Gospel.* The Lord invites all men to himself. He freely invites them to come to him as they are and not because of anything good or righteous they may find in themselves. The sinner does not look to see if he has worthiness, or if there are preliminary signs of grace in him. We should be free, flexible and fervent in our preaching of the free offers of the Gospel. In other words we must not in any way be stiff or starched or hampered. If the doctrines of grace hamper the preacher in any way it indicates that he has not grasped their implications. The Puritans can help us a very great deal here.[4] They were marvellously free. They held the doctrines of grace; they held to particular redemption absolutely, but this never hampered them in their preaching of the free offers of the Gospel. There is great joy in offering the Gospel, because the Holy Spirit often favours Scripture passages containing Gospel invitations and applies them with power to sinners.

(v) *Faith in preaching.* Do we have faith in the Word of God as such? It is possible for the preacher to become over-worked or distracted and without realizing it he loses faith in his own preaching as God's instrument not only of edification but of conversion. He needs to pray always for the power of the Holy Spirit in preaching. Do we really believe that the Word of God is powerful, sharper than any two-edged sword (Heb. 4:12)? Do we have a great faith in the Word of God preached? Do we believe in the Holy Ghost sent down from heaven when we preach? Do we expect for the Holy Ghost, God himself, to come down from heaven? That is what Peter said (1 Pet. 1:12), and Paul declared that "our Gospel unto you came not in word only, but also in power and in the Holy Ghost and in much assurance" (1 Thess. 1:5). We should wrestle with the Lord that he will send down the Holy Ghost and that there will be much assurance and power in the preaching. We should do this every time we preach, not just sometimes. W. G. T. Shedd has a fine sermon with the title, "The certain success of Evangelistic Labour," in which he says, "suppose that I myself have never felt the revolutionising power of Christianity, or have never seen an instance of it in another person: will not the theoretical belief that I may have in this religion be likely to wane away in the lapse of time? If a power is not exerted, we begin to doubt its existence. And if an individual or church witnesses no effusions of the Spirit, and no actual conversions of the human soul, it will inevitably begin to query whether there be any Holy Ghost, and whether the Gospel is anything more than ethics."[5]

It is the effusions of the Holy Spirit that we long for. It is conversions which we look for, pray for, plead for and aim at. The regeneration of souls is the best proof we have of the power of God among us.

Shedd goes on to illustrate this from different parts of history. The beginning of the eighteenth century was a time of scepticism, doubt, coldness and rationalism, and one of the reasons was that there were not these powerful conversions. But when the awakening came what a change there was then! God was in the land. People were being converted from all strata of society. Rationalism crumpled like paper. We need such spiritual awakening today. It will show itself in preaching first just as it did with the apostles. And if we look behind powerful preaching we will see the Spirit of grace and supplication.

5. A dynamic communication of the Gospel to every creature
My headings with regard to the above are as follows: (i) The prayer meeting; (ii) effective house to house visiting; (iii) relevance in our presenta-

tion of truth; (iv) using our homes as a base; (v) the use of literature; (vi) zeal and perseverance in the work. All these aspects are connected to, spring from, are inspired by or directed by the local church.

(i) *The prayer meeting.* Prayer is fundamental to the activity of evangelism. This is obvious but nevertheless requires assertion. All too often the primary place of prayer is forgotten or added as a postscript after human organization has dominated, and human wisdom dictated the details of a project. The New Testament not only urges the importance of prayer (Eph. 6:18) but this is evident in the lives of the apostles. Acts 4:13-32 is one instance of many that could be quoted.

By its very nature prayer is a reminder that salvation belongs to God. There will be no salvation but such as he is pleased to give. As we have seen, our major weapon is preaching. God pours out his regenerating power through preaching. Such preaching cannot be taken for granted. It has to be sought by preacher and people. Paul appeals to the Ephesians to pray for him that utterance will be given to him (Eph. 6:19).

Prayer is essential if we are to receive spiritual vitality and drive to persevere in the work of evangelism which means perseverance in our interest in people and contact with them. Wisdom and ability, guidance and insight are born through prayer as the details are laid before the Lord. The church needs to gather for prayer at least twice a week in order that there will be adequate opportunity to include the responsibilities and details of evangelistic endeavour in the prayer life of the church.

Some have tended to think that the amount of prayer is the crucial factor as though God will be conned into action by the force of numbers or by repetition. Such notions are misguided. The intelligent, enlightened prayer of one righteous man can be worth more than ten thousand prayers that are not according to the truth.

(ii) *Effective house to house visiting.* It goes without saying that every country and area is different when it comes to actual opportunities to present the Gospel. Open-air preaching may be feasible in one country but be quite ineffective in another. We find that our community for the most part is shut in with television sets and families tend to live to themselves. Opportunities to use the mass media for evangelism are few and far between. Open-air preaching tends to be drowned by the roar of traffic and the general attitude of the public is to despise such attempts and ignore them. Under these circumstances house to house visiting, if thoughtfully conducted, is found in most cases to be by far the best means of evangelism. To evangelize is to teach and instruct every creature in the Gospel (Matt. 28:19). The suitability of visiting every home with that in mind should be apparent.

It is advisable that only those who are well-equipped in knowledge and have a gift to approach people should be encouraged. Visiting can be done two by two but where a man is experienced he can visit with greater effectiveness on his own particularly on a Saturday when the men-folk are at home. It is not suitable for men to visit women on their own. One purpose of visiting is to make contact with the people and to inform them of the work of the church in their area. While people are invited to come it is to be realised that it is exceedingly unlikely that they will respond to such an invitation and therefore a main objective must be to broach the fundamental issues of the Gospel. We are to go and teach or disciple all peoples where they are and not wait for them to come to us, for we will wait in vain!

Commonsense plays a major role in house to house visiting. Records should be kept. Diligent follow up work is vital. Suitable times need to be chosen for the visitation, and so on.

(iii) *Relevance in our presentation of truth.* If a church is well instructed and the believers have assimilated the Gospel, and practise it daily, this is going to be the most telling factor in evangelism. Instead of thinking of the Gospel as a simple formula they will be ready to show the relevance of the Gospel to every area of life; the family, employment, civil law, politics, recreation, ecology, the state of institutional churches, the moral law, education, evolution, the existence of Israel and the Jews, the question of famine and undeveloped countries, etc. A well instructed Christian will be able to converse on all these matters and it is by the power of the Spirit that the essential matters of personal repentance and faith are introduced and discussed.

The question of apologetics is inescapable in evangelism. Here again the pulpit occupies a central role. If a Christian thinks that the natural man is neutral and that he is in a position to make judgments about the Bible and about God then this will cripple evangelism. Also if he thinks that it is helpful to impress unbelievers with the glamour of the Church such as some pop stars professing to be Christians then he is wasting time because the Church can never be glamorous in the sense that the world is glamorous. The natural man is not led to conviction and an inward change by showing that Christianity is nice and easy and not very different from the world. It should always be borne in mind that if there is no conviction of sin there will be no conversion; if there is no repentance there will be no salvation!

(iv) *Using our homes as a base.* In the early Church there was no other possibility but for believers to meet in homes. Outsiders are more ready to join us in a domestic atmosphere than in an ecclesiastical one, especially when church going is completely out of vogue. When a meeting is due to take place in a certain road, it is good to concentrate on visiting all the people in that road and extending invitations where there seems to be any possibility of acceptance.

It is also helpful to visit a Christian home if such exists in a particular locality where we are visiting and have prayer first before actually going

54

to knock on doors. Afterwards the details of the visiting with that Christian family should be shared in order that further contact may be encouraged.

(v) *The use of literature.* John Bunyan in his fascinating book, "The Holy War", shows how Diabolus overcame the city of Mansoul through Eargate and Eyegate. Likewise when Emmanuel, the Captain of our Salvation came to make his conquest over fallen Mansoul, he too came through Eargate and Eyegate. Literature has its place but it is greatly inferior to the personal approach in which words and expressions are adapted in an ideal way to a living situation. In our society the value of mass distribution of literature along impersonal lines is questionable. Literature does, however, have an important place when following up contacts especially if items are carefully and thoughtfully selected in order to be suitable to personal problems that have come to light in conversation.

(vi) *Zeal and perseverance in the work.* To make a start in house to house evangelism is difficult enough but to persevere can be even more exacting. The best motives will be needed to sustain determination and perseverance.

There is surely no higher motive than that of the great commission. Our Lord commanded us to teach all nations and assured us that he was with us even to the end of time. If he has commanded evangelism and promised to be with us, then that ought to be enough to spur us on. However, there are many other motives to encourage us, including the promise that the Holy Spirit will convince the world of sin, of righteousness and of judgment. The doctrine of Election is also very heartening as we know that the Father has a people which he will give to his Son and that success must crown the right use of means. Compassion is a powerful motive for evangelism. The more we are conformed to Christ the more we will be like him in goodness, compassion and concern toward his enemies (Luke 23:24).

I conclude by urging that we should go out of our way to encourage one another in the urgent and essential task of evangelism.

REFERENCES

[1]It is questionable whether Paul is speaking of sound teaching when he refers to "gold, silver and precious stones". 1 Cor. 3:11-15. The foundation has already been laid, as we see in Matt. 16:18, Eph. 2:21, 22, and particularly 1 Pet. 2:5. We are built on that foundation. Wood, hay and stubble represent those who are false converts—the unregenerate; gold, silver and precious stones, those who are true. This passage is a vindication of the gathered church principle and the necessity of discipline with regard to a realistic church membership. R. L. Dabney in an exposition of this passage warns against the use of artificial means to gain professions of faith. c.f. *Discussions*, Vol. 1, p. 551 ff. [2]*Banner of Truth* No. 48, p. 8. [3]*Reformation Today* No. 18. *Finney and the disappearance of revival* by Clive Tyler. [4] In a paper, *The Puritan Approach to Persuading Souls*, given at the Westminster (Puritan) Conference the question of the free offer is expounded in detail. It is published in a booklet with the title *Adding to the Church* at 50 pence and is available from Carey Publications. [5]W. G. T. Shedd, *Sermons to the Spiritual Man*, Banner of Truth, p. 413.

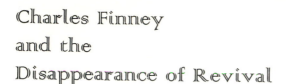

Charles Finney and the Disappearance of Revival

Clive Tyler

SOME TWENTY YEARS AGO, PROGRESSIVE ENGLISH CHURCHMEN WERE horrified to discover that mass evangelism was again raising its head! They had assumed that its effective life had died out with Moody and Sankey, Torrey and Alexander. Evangelicals, on the other hand, hailed the crusades as a sign of renewed life and blessing for the Church: with a heightening of interest generally, considerable numbers were converted. Many saw the movement as the answer to the churches' apathy and to the increasing godlessness of Britain. At the same time a prominent preacher who had himself experienced revival viewed the crusades with some misgivings, suggesting that the resultant blessing would effectively mask the depth of the real problem. It was suggested that genuine revival would be delayed for at least ten years. It was replied that evangelism could supply the solution as well as old fashioned revival.

At this distance in time we can assess more easily the true situation, and we can see clearly that for all the apparent blessing received, mass evangelism—or "revivalism"—has been quite unable to stem the increasing tide of unbelief, secularism and the wickedness and evil arising in the Western world. Some still continue to see the answer as more efficient mass evangelism of the crusade type; others look to renewal through the baptism of the Holy Spirit and the Charismatic movement, and yet a third group claims that nothing less than a "Holy Ghost Revival" in the historic mould will meet the need. While agreeing with the necessity of true revival a fourth group (including the editors of *Reformation Today*) increasingly see the necessity of reformation in doctrine, practice and experience.

Strangely, the first three emphases come into focus in the figure of Charles Finney and many in each of these three groups look to him as the mentor. "The Father of Modern Evangelism," "The Father of the Modern Soul Saving Movement". Popularly it is claimed that he saved American church life and evangelism from the dead orthodoxy of the early nineteenth century and that his approach can save the twentieth century Church from its present malaise. His official biographer, Miller, wrote: "His *Lectures on Revivals of Religion* have been to the blessing of millions and constitute the hope for the present day". He goes on: "his was a marvellous life to the converting of half a million souls," and he speaks of the blessing received during his ministry as, "unparalleled since the days of the apostles". The prominent place that Finney holds is undoubtedly deserved and though many of the assessments made of his work are grossly overstated and superficial we soon realise, when we come to grips with him, what a profound effect he has had upon the Church worldwide. It should be stressed therefore that this subject is of more than academic interest. Finney's teaching and methodology are all-pervasive. In some ways he is a far greater influence in practice than Karl Barth. Moreover few lives in history show more clearly the interrelation between theology and practice, and how a theological idea may radically change the evangelistic methods of the Church throughout the earth.

Finney's Life Marks a Watershed in Church History

A man of tremendous personality, force, and perhaps genius, Finney represents in belief and practice a bridge between the old religious world and the new. The great changes working themselves out in nineteenth century history became embodied in his life and experiences. He was a symptom of the changing times.

Theologically the old world of Reformed historical Christianity was behind him: the world where the Bible was the word from the mouth of the living God, infallible and inerrant in which was to be found the sole authority for the beliefs and practices of Christians. Before him lay the new world with its modern approach to Scripture, an approach in which man is the judge of the Bible's trustworthiness and value: a world of criticism and rationalism where the plain teaching of Scripture can be rejected if it cuts across enlightened reason! This critical and rationalistic spirit can be clearly seen in embryo in the young Finney. It is no accident, but rather significant and symptomatic that in his major work, *Lectures on Systematic Theology,* the first two hundred pages are largely philosophical discussion with a mere handful of references to Scripture. It is as unlike the older biblically based systematic theologies as it is like the philosophical theologies of the modern church. Finney is the turning point. Behind him are the doctrines of historic Christianity, before him the world of liberalism and the autonomy of man. Preceding him are the evangelical and Reformed doctrines of the faith embodied in the Canons of Dort, the Thirty-Nine Articles, the Westminster Confession and the other, great credal confessions. These Finney rejected. For him they misunderstood Scripture. What was already beginning to be called the New Divinity, New School Theology, or Taylorism was adopted and propagated by Finney as Gospel truth. To this extent he made common cause with Liberalism and Modernism and led the way to the undoctrinal and untheological evangelism of the latter part of the last century, which in this present century has become much more accentuated.

This severance with the old doctrine led inevitably to a change in practice. The practice before Finney was of Biblical evangelism, where the Church's methods were controlled by and subjected to the dictates of Scripture. It is significant, surely, that the modern Church is largely ignorant of the history of evangelism before Moody and Sankey. The pragmatic approach, rampant in American life, where anything that got results was commended, was applied to evangelistic endeavour. It is universally admitted that the pioneer in the new methods was Charles Finney. Says his biographer Miller: "He was the innovator, he was the bringer in of the new measures". He led the van for Moody and Sankey, Billy Sunday and even for the aberrations of Amy Semple MacPherson and Marjoe. These are his lineal descendants. Quantity becomes the great mark of success. We are told, for example, that whereas certain skilful evangelists can expect in America to lead a soul to Christ in 35 minutes, it takes two or three hours in Britain! The old methods of evangelism so blessed by God appear to have suffered the same fate as craftsmanship, being driven out by mass production. Nowadays the old ways are hardly recognised to be evangelism at all, and those who speak out for love of truth against pragmatic and psychological evangelism are likely to be pilloried as opponents of God and salvation. This is exactly how Finney reacted to those who criticised his new measures in the nineteenth century. He claimed they were hyper-Calvinists, spiritually dead and unconcerned for men's souls whereas the ministries and testimonies of these men bore eloquent proof to the contrary.

The confusion as to what evangelism and the Gospel ought to be is due not only to ignorance of Church history, but, more seriously, to a dislike of Biblical exposition and doctrine of apostolic evangelism.

To put the whole matter in perspective it will help us to examine Finney's early life and experience and see how it was interwoven with his theology.

Finney's Early Life and Christian Experience

Born in 1792, Charles Finney was brought up in the centre of New York State. The prevailing theological view of the churches in the area seems to have been Princetonian Calvinism. Finney suggests in his auto-biography that he grew up with little opportunity to hear the Gospel, but this seems unlikely. In a paper on Finney (to which I am much indebted) given at the Puritan Conference, Paul Cook maintains that we are to treat Finney's comments about this with caution. Finney's account was written late in life and seems to be an interpretation of the facts in the light of his later theological position. Finney claims, for example, that the churches were almost all hyper-Calvinistic and that there was little evidence of spiritual life and zeal until he commenced his labours. This is far from the truth. There had been many revivals before Finney's day and those involved were invariably distinctively Reformed in their doctrinal position. These revivals were still in evidence prior to Finney's conversion. There is no doubt whatsoever that Jefferson County near the St. Lawrence River, where Finney came as a newly qualified young lawyer, had seen successive revivals for years. Gale, the young pastor of the church which Finney began to attend out of "professional interest", had seen 65 people converted in the early months of his ministry there.

Charles Finney was converted two years after this in 1821 and he interprets the experience as being due almost wholly to an effort of his own will and resolution. "I made up my mind that I would settle the question of my soul's salvation at once." [2] This is in accord with his later theological position, as though the experience were divorced from any external influences and due only to his own willingness. Yet in spite of Finney's interpretation the sovereignty of God seems marked indeed. "My conscience was awakened, I had a great shame for sin, my mind was enlightened, I had a vision of Christ and I was broken down under an outpouring of the Spirit." That certainly does not sound like a purely subjective experience but rather God at work in power. Despite the impression he gives, it would appear that the prayers of his mother and his sweetheart, as well as the preaching of Pastor Gale and the prayer meetings he attended, were all instruments in the hands of God leading to his conversion.

His friend, A. T. Pierson, described Finney as ". . . a born reformer, impassioned to the borders of impetuosity, positive to the borders of bigotry and original to the borders of heresy." [3]

With this temperament, a legal training, acute mental ability and the physical energy of the backwoodsman, he commenced his Christian life. A novice in theological understanding, he soon came into conflict with the Biblical and Reformed theology of George Gale, the minister. To Finney, Gale's was a false theology. As a lawyer he objected to it on rational and pragmatic grounds. He felt it to be inhibiting in practice.

59

The classic Westminster Confession of Faith he arrogantly dismissed. "Dogmas . . . sustained for the most part by passages of Scripture that were totally irrelevant, and not in a single instance sustained by passages which, in a court of law, would have been considered at all conclusive."[4] Here we see a novice, self-opinionated and puffed up. He refused to accept Gale's views on the atonement, regeneration, faith, repentance, and the slavery of the will. When it is remembered that these are the historic evangelical doctrines, not peripheral matters, but central, pivotal fundamentals of the faith, we realise how serious a division there was.

Paul Cook points out that the key to the situation is that Finney attributes infallibility to the human reason: ". . . there can be no error in the *a priori* intuitions of reason"[5] even in matters of religion. This is the crux of his whole theology.

Finney's Theology

It is not easy to set out Finney's early views with exactness, for his systematic treatment came later in life. Nevertheless, the essential characteristics of his Pelagianism were clearly present in his disputation with Gale and were to be developed later with logical precision in his

Lectures on Systematic Theology.

Like modern theologians such as Karl Barth he uses scriptural terms and classic phraseology, but gives them new meanings. He speaks of "justification", "repentance" and "faith", but the words are devalued and debased in content.

Sin

In his view of sin, Finney assumes, firstly, that moral qualities attach only to *deliberate* acts. Men are not sinners by nature, they are sinners because they commit sins. He refused to accept that dispositions and states of nature may be in themselves sinful. For him it followed that love, malice, hatred, etc., are non moral, neither good nor bad in themselves.

A second assumption is that there is no depravity attached to the human constitution as such. Pure will and external temptations are the only real factors in sinfulness. Finney could not fail to recognise the universal moral depravity of the world however, and he suggests that this is due to the effect of the world on the weak human physical (not moral) constitution of man. Children, when they come into the world, are like little animals. They are neutral with a non-moral nature. (Thus, a child dying in infancy has no need of the grace of God or the atoning work of Christ.) Only when they are old enough to make moral judgements, to deliberately will, do they become moral beings and at that point they become morally depraved.[6]

The fact that all children exhibit moral depravity is attributed to their weakened physical constitution received from their parents, it is this that makes them prone to self-gratification, though in itself not sinful. Finney believed that a few generations on a correct diet (he was a strong advocate of a Grahamic diet—no meat, tea, coffee or other injurious substances) would remove these physical defects from mankind. Clearly for Finney there is no place for the doctrine of original sin, of the imputation of Adam's guilt to all his progeny or of the corruption of the human heart from birth onwards. There is, in fact, no "heart" at all in this view of things, for he gives it a sense only equivalent to *will*.[7] Man, then, is good or bad only insofar as his actions are unselfish or not; he is not sinful in his own being. We do well to note a most serious divergence from Scripture here, for in Scripture holiness and unholiness attach to the person himself as an intelligent moral creature.

Thirdly, Finney assumes that man is always neutral—everywhere and always he has a plenary and inalienable ability to obey God in everything he demands, that is, obligation implies ability. Here we are led to the very core of Finney's theological system. It actually arose out of an espousal of the philosophical theories of the German, Dr. Immanuel Kant. Paul Cook pertinently describes the first lecture in the Systematic Theology as a "hotch-potch" of Kantian philosophy, particularly in this emphasis on "I ought, therefore I can". In its exact theological form, Finney's theological system appears to be very close to the New School Divinity of N. W. Taylor, which was the old heresy of Pelagius, in modern dress. Pelagius is the true father of all these children. Jerome described Pelagianism as the first organised system of self salvation taught in the Church.

Regeneration

Finney's doctrine of salvation is built up on the foundation of obligation implying ability. We are commanded to be born again, therefore we must be able to do this.[8] Regeneration, in his thinking (and how modern is this emphasis), becomes no more than a radical change of intention. There is no real change of heart or nature. No renewal and revival of the depraved constitution, merely a change of will and this is wholly within man's natural power. He says in one passage: "We are saved by free grace drawing and securing the concurrence of the will" (John 6:44). On examination, we discover with B. B. Warfield that "drawing" is simply illumination or teaching, nothing more than better motivation or argument to move the sinner's will. God's power is limited to persuasion. Using Finney's own illustration, God's ability to draw men is akin to a statesman swaying the Senate by argument, or an advocate addressing the jury.[9] (He describes the evangelist's task in the same terms!) The only power available to God is the power to motivate. This is a far cry from the sovereign act of an omnipotent God, which constitutes Biblical regeneration. It is also a far cry from the dragging in of the net which is the point of John 6:44: "No man can come to me except the Father drag (draw A.V.) him". In Finney's teaching there is no divine transforming energy, merely better communication! God speaks continually in the hope that man will consent, he can do no more. Finney reasons that in any case we need nothing more, for all are able to repent and, when sufficiently motivated, will do so. There is no barrier whatsoever except selfish desires. "At any moment man can put these away," he says, "and turn to Christ." Salvation becomes, therefore, little more than a change of purpose, or commitment to a new way—it is a human action. This is plainly contrary to Scripture where the new birth, or regeneration, is wholly the work of God, and this is why Finney and those who follow his views speak of consecration, or commitment, or surrender rather than of regeneration. In contemporary fashion he confuses regeneration and conversion. "We regenerate ourselves"—only the man can alter his choice.[10] "Sinners can go to hell," he says, "in spite of God, neither God nor any other being can regenerate him if he will not turn."[11] How great a divergence this is from the Biblical approach where repentance and faith are gifts of God, and where men cry to God to turn them that they might turn to Him. Finney fails to see that conversion is the outward effect of the inward, imparted, divine life, for his view is that the work of the Holy Spirit is external and limited.

Justification

So far as justification is concerned, Finney could not logically have such a doctrine, since he had no doctrine of depravity. If there is no imputed guilt, there is no need of Christ's imputed righteousness. He rejects the Reformation view that justification is a forensic act on the grounds of Christ's atoning work upon the cross. He says quite plainly: "The doctrine of an imputed righteousness, or that Christ's obedience to the law was accounted as our obedience, is founded on a most false and nonsensical assumption." In his view the sinner is not declared just but is treated as just by amnesty. Finney was well aware that he contradicted Augustinian soteriology at almost every point, and that his doctrine of depravity led him to deny and ignore classic Reformed teaching. For him, Christ's death shows us what God is like as a moral governor. The death of Christ becomes more a means of legal satisfaction than a vicarious atonement. One searches in vain for emphasis on expiation, or propitiation. Moreover, it is interesting to see that his modern disciples take his theology to its logical conclusion, and in so doing make common cause with liberal views of salvation, in refusing to speak of the wrath of God against depravity and sin, while proclaiming an all-loving God unable to do more for sinners than plead that they use their will aright. Such theology is man-centred rather than God-centred.

Sanctification

Moving on to sanctification, he argues somewhat along these lines: if a man comes to God in repentance and faith—that is, he turns his will, or changes his choice, for these terms hold no other meaning for Finney than this—God freely pardons all his past sin. This act of "regeneration" he regards as "an entire present change . . . from entire sinfulness to entire holiness . . . (leading to) . . . full obedience for the time being, after which it is only a question of maintenance."[12] That is, regeneration brings one into a state of present sinlessness or, if you will, perfect sanctification. This change is a single act, because repentance involves a total change of choice. Thus his first righteous act is also his last, for he becomes entirely holy.[13] For Finney, the moment a man was converted he ceased to be a sinner—all his sinful acts were forgiven. As there was no sinful nature, and therefore no basis from which sin could spring, the man must be perfect. "At this point," says Benjamin Warfield, "we are astonished to discover that this perfect Christian, according to Finney, can backslide!" This, however, is logical because if the man has the natural ability, when he wills, to turn to Christ, then he may also reject Christ at will. He becomes a religious yo-yo—up and down, in and out of the Kingdom of Heaven at will. When Finney speaks of "backsliding" it has the real significance of apostasy, since it is a total act. Man must begin all over again; there is the coming out at the second meeting, the third, fourth and so on. In his actual practice we discover that this was the effect of the preaching of his gospel. His converts fell continually. It is no accident that they knew little peace, stability and assurance. These cannot be known outside of a true grasp and experience of justification by faith. How can there be assurance of salvation, if all depends on capricious, human choice rather than the sovereign will and work of God? As J. C. Ryle put it, "There can be no assurance for Arminians," and we may add even less for the products of Finney's Pelagian gospel. Again, the effects of his man-centred approach are everywhere to be seen in the modern evangelistic scene, where his ideas and methods prevail. There is little stability, peace and assurance and despite "total surrender", "total availability", etc., there is little evidence of solid, Biblical, holy living either.

His Ministry and Revival Methods

Soon after his conversion experience he began to exercise a powerful influence in the locality, and he was soon to be found within the bounds of the Christian ministry. He approached the elders of the local presbytery, knowing full well that much of what he believed flatly contradicted the stated constitutional beliefs of the Presbyterian Church. The elders, nevertheless, accepted him, since his obvious zeal and energy for Christ's cause, coupled with his remarkable conversion experience, led them to fear to deny him entrance lest they should hinder God's work; and, says Finney, because they were confused over the New School Divinity which was coming into fashion, they refused to ask him questions about his theology. It may be that they were timid in the face of his personal force and precocity. In this way he entered into his ministerial vows. Someone, commenting later, said that it is interesting that he should regard coffee drinking as a serious sin, and yet be so unconcerned about dishonesty and broken ministerial vows. (There are, of course, modern parallels.)

Immediately after his ordination in 1823 he began itinerant preaching, causing division and schism wherever he went for the next two years. This was due in part at least, to his own attitude and spirit, which were so severely critical and censorious of all efforts to evangelise but his own. He set up a reaction amongst the ministers of churches, whom he then dubbed dead and hyper-Calvinistic. At the same time, he was working during a season of unusual blessing as a result of the Holy Spirit's work and we must not overlook or discount the fact that he with others enjoyed the blessings of rains from heaven and fruitful harvests of an order that has not been witnessed for over a hundred years. He laboured in the context of revival. It appears to me that the problems arose when Finney endeavoured to impose his own ideas and methods on God's work, instead of following the leading of Scripture and the Holy Spirit. He believed that his work as an evangelist involved stirring up men to choice and action—this was the distinctive characteristic of his ministry and the most significant element for the future. He moved to the west of New York State and immediately commenced a remarkable work known today as the Western Revivals.[14] He deliberately set out to promote excitement, to stir the area by impassioned preaching, for which he had great ability. It appears that Finney took the expertise of a talented lawyer, unsubdued by Christian experience and immediately pressed into service in the headstrong manner of the novice. We find today that the new convert, who is an expert in some field—Freudian psychology, business tycoon, pop star, opera-singing, weight-lifting, ballet teaching—on being converted is encouraged to use all and every technique for witness. Whether it be Pop or Rock music, or modern high pressure salesmanship, it is used uncritically and rashly, out of harmony with the Gospel it desires to promote. Finney's approach was without doubt one of force,[15] his method being denunciation of the most violent kind, bordering on defamation. It is strange that Finney, who argued so strongly that God could only work by love and persuasion and not coercion, should find it necessary to exert pressure which God could not. The explanation lies in his understanding of the work of the advocate. It is the advocate's task to turn the jury's mind, to sway the jury in his client's favour. The members of the jury are free to choose as they will, and they must come to their decision before the case is over. This approach was brought in to serve gospel ends. It was Finney's deliberate policy to break down the will of his hearers. Since they could turn if they would, a battle resulted between the preacher

64

and the will to make it turn. To that end he used every possible means —coarse and violent language, the anxious seat, suitable music, the protracted appeal, and many other means which came to be regarded as the "new measures". This met with considerable opposition, naturally, since the approach was almost wholly novel in the history of evangelism, and Finney engaged in powerful polemics against the opposition, claiming that they were fighting God.

As to the results of his work, there are two sides to the picture. "Flood tides of revival glory," said his biographer, Miller, were seen in the Rochester revivals, 10,000 were converted in one meeting, the whole city converted by 1832 and hundreds of thousands were gathered in the complete series of Western Revivals (1825-32). One finds other writers lauding the success in similar terms, but there is serious misrepresentation, for they fail to stress the situation as it was a few years after! Dr. A. B. Dod writing in 1835 said: "It is now generally understood that the numerous converts of the new measures have been in most cases like the morning cloud and the early dew. In some places, not a fifth or even a tenth part of them remain."[16] Those who did remain were a constant source of trouble in the churches, being fanatical, discontented and censorious. Dod was decidedly against Finney and his work. He was of the Princetonian School and he found many pastors, evangelists and revival leaders to stand with him against the new measures. This then might well be dismissed as a biased judgement. B. B. Warfield gives, however, a number of comments from Finney's close friends and fellow labourers. James Boyle writing to Finney in 1834: "I have revisited many of these fields (where we laboured) and groaned in spirit to see the sad, frigid, casual, contentious state into which the churches had fallen"[17]—this written three months after Finney had left. Asa Mahan, Finney's fellow worker and close friend for the whole of his life, tells us that everyone who was concerned in these revivals suffered a sad, subsequent lapse; the people were left like a dead coal which could not be reignited; the pastors were shorn of all their spiritual power and all of the evangelists, with the exception of brother Finney and father Nash, became quite unfit to be evangelists and pastors. Finney himself said, "I was able to bring many to temporary repentance and faith!" He said again in 1835, "They soon relapse into their former state". In his Systematic Theology he confesses that the greater number of his "converts" were a disgrace to religion. As for the lasting aspect the results in the churches were disastrous.

If it is true that there were genuine revivals up to 1832, then after 1832 there were none. Churches burned up with false fire had become terrified of the true fire of the Spirit, and his work was quenched. In 1832 the opposition was so fierce that Finney moved to a New York City Church where he began to set out his *Lectures on Revivals of Religion* as an apologia for his novel methods. Through this work his personal fame and the methods he employed spread throughout the evangelical world.

The immediate effects of this Pelagian gospel ran true to type, with temporary excitement, and temporary decisions which tended to fade when the external stimulus was withdrawn. A more lasting effect was in the area of sanctification, the creation of a whole new class of religious people who now made their appearance in Church history as the "carnal" Christians. They had made a profession and there had been an external change, but they now bore all the marks of the worldly man. Finney claims that the reason for this state of affairs was that he did not preach sanctification enough. Though some attempt has been made to comment on Finney's doctrine of sanctification, it is not at all clear what he really believed on the matter. He says quite properly that all good in man is due to the indwelling Christ; from first to last it is the Spirit's work and it is not by works of the law. (He was too good a Pelagian however to admit quietism and he leaves a large place for human endeavour, even to the point, in practice, of legalism.) It does appear that *enlightenment* by the indwelling Christ and not divine power was the means of sanctification. He says that we do not need Christ's strength, as we have sufficient of our own,[18] but what we do need is inducement. At the end of his life he flirted for a time with Oberlin perfectionism of Mahan's type; "perfection" being "complete righteousness which is adjusted to fluctuating ability". Mahan, his fellow worker at Oberlin, published his views on the baptism of the Holy Spirit, and for a time Finney espoused similar views and his letters on this subject were published in a popular and influential book, *Power from on High,* in which he defines the baptism of power as the ability to fasten saving impressions on the minds of men, as did the apostles at Pentecost. He is thinking here of his early experiences in the Revivals, when a single look from the evangelist was sufficient to break down souls and to lead them to conversion. In modern terms, Finney had charisma.

Warfield's comment is pertinent here. "If it is not the Word but the preacher that is the power of God unto Salvation, the evangelist has become a Sacrament." The evangelist, not the word preached, is now the key to the situation. It is not so much the clarity of the message as the personality of the messenger which counts. "It is interesting," says Warfield again, "that the God who cannot work alone is now aided by the supernatural evangelist." It may well be that Finney, at the end of his long life tragically was looking for some such power as had been lost in 1832, when the Spirit departed.

The Legacy of his Teaching and Methods

The long term effects were immense. Due to the widespread acceptance of his ideas, religion became increasingly man-centred, for his gospel was anthropocentric even though he began in the midst of genuine religious revival. The age in which we live is almost wholly man-centred and God appears strangely unwilling to work with us. It is no accident that the popular liberal and progressive theologies are also humanistic, for here again there is a basic Pelagian tendency. In consequence, preaching is persuasion, not teaching, and often degenerates into scolding. Men can turn by their own ability and they won't! In some of the worst forms of preaching Christ is reduced to the level of a beggar pleading pathetically to get into a man's house. By losing sight of Christ's power to reveal himself to whomsoever he will (Matt. 11:27) and of sinners' inability and spiritual impotence, the true nature of the free offers of the Gospel is destroyed. It is no longer a question of salvation by God's power but rather, "I will save myself when I feel like it."

More serious still is the effect upon revivals of religion. In the time of Jonathan Edwards, a revival was regarded as a supernatural and miraculous work of the sovereign Holy Spirit, to be prayed down from heaven. By the time Finney's lectures had leavened their way into the Church, revival had become something for man to promote and work up. It is significant that his apologia for his methods of promoting revivals is based on his psychology of man rather than on the teaching of Scripture.

Finney began in revival and ended with organised "revivalism". He began in revival and he ended up with modern evangelism. For the most part the Church has continued in that line ever since. Today one reads in American literature: "Don't have your revival until you have seen samples of our colour posters." Or, more dramatically: "Revivals arranged, results guaranteed; terms moderate!" It is possible to subscribe to a correspondence course on Finney's methods, at the end of which one is qualified to have a revival!

We have come in the twentieth century to think automatically in terms of new methods and new measures, instead of a new, wholehearted turning to God in repentance and faith with a genuine recognition of our total inability as sinners to do God's work for him. The absence of revival from God is a matter of grief. Is it true that so long as we continue to rely on man we continue to grieve the Spirit and hinder the return of revival? Is it true that we neglect the urgent need of reformation at our peril? Surely this whole subject is of momentous importance for us today.

REFERENCES

1 "Finney on Revival." Paper given by Paul Cook at the Puritan Conference, London, and published with the title *One Steadfast High Intent*, p. 5. 2 *Memoirs of C. G. Finney written by himself*, 1876, chap. 2. 3 A. T. Pierson, *Evangelistic Work*, 1892, p. 140 (quoted by P. Cook). 4 Finney: *Autobiography*, pp. 45 ff. 5 *Ibid.*, pp. 6 ff. 6 Finney: *Lectures on Systematic Theology*, 1851, pp. 388 ff. 7 B. B. Warfield. *Perfectionism*, 1958 (Presbyterian and Reformed), pp. 179 f. 8 *Ibid.*, op. cit.,

p. 173.   9 Finney. *Sermons on Important Subjects,* p. 30.   Cf. Warfield, p. 175.
10 Cook, see above, p. 9 also Finney *Lectures on Systematic Theology,* pp. 411 ff.
11 B. B. Warfield, op. cit., p. 193.   12 Finney, *Lectures on Systematic Theology,* pp.
593 and 537.   13 B. B. Warfield, op. cit., pp. 203 f.   14 Finney, *Memoirs,* p. 144.
15 Fowler, *Historical Sketch of Presbyterianism.*   1877, p. 264.   16 A. B. Dod.
Princeton Review, 1847, p. 141.   17 B. B. Warfield, op. cit., pp. 26 ff.   18 *Ibid.,* p. 193.
Finney, *Systematic Theology,* p. 693.

John Calvin the Pastor

Jim van Zyl

OF THE MANY TOWERING FIGURES IN THE HISTORY OF THE CHRISTIAN Church, John Calvin is probably the most maligned and misunderstood. Much has been written about his brilliance as a theologian, and this is undoubtedly true. One has only to read his *magnum opus, The Institutes of the Christian Religion*, to see that. It is quite wrong, however, to categorize his theology as something cold, academic and forbidding. Only the uninformed could talk in this way. Even a cursory reading of his works will reveal, immediately, how deeply and warmly he writes and speaks of the things of God.

Again, much criticism has been directed against his logical mind and his lawyer's ability. He was too much of a machine in his dealing with men and God's Truth, so the criticism runs. It is certainly true that Calvin was a trained lawyer, trained under Pierre de L'Estoile, one of the finest French lawyers of his day, but it must never be forgotten that Calvin used his logic almost exclusively in the service of God's Church, and never as an end in itself, much less for his own glory. One of the finest examples of this occurred in neighbouring Lausanne in October, 1536, only a few months after Calvin's entry into Geneva. During a religious debate, at which Calvin and others were present, the topic of the Lord's Supper came up for discussion. Angered by the ignorance of Mimard, one of 174 Roman priests who had accused the Reformers of holding the teachings of Augustine and the Church Fathers in low esteem, Calvin stood up and, without any books or manuscripts before him, proceeded to quote and expound from the Fathers in such a manner as to set the opposition reeling. So powerful was Calvin's refutation that a well known priest, Jean Tandy, stood up, confessed that he had sinned against the Spirit, was denouncing his priesthood and would henceforth ". . . follow Christ and his pure doctrine alone . . .".[1] So much for Calvin's *cold* logic! To a right use of logic Calvin added scholarship. Jean Cadier, quoting from Luchesius Smits, points out that Smits ". . . has discovered in the Reformer's writings 1,700 actual quotations from St. Augustine and 2,400 references, a fact which shows an extremely thorough acquaintance with Augustine's work".[2]

Perhaps the most perverted image that has come down to us through the centuries has been that of Calvin the dictator and tyrant of Geneva. The following quotations will highlight this assessment of Calvin. Newman says: "As a thoroughgoing theocrat, Calvin was necessarily and on principle a persecutor".[3] Daniel-Rops goes even further when he says: ". . . The atmosphere in Geneva during these astonishing years almost defies the imagination. It was that of a régime of 'public safety' in the most complete and rigorous sense of the term . . . a reign of terror was established; but in Geneva its horror was aggravated by the fact that it was founded on religious principles . . . the rigidity and apparent cruelty of his theocratic dictatorship".[4]

These wild allegations can be refuted but I hope, as we look at the reformer as a pastor, we may see some sort of balance restored and justice done to the real figure of Calvin. We shall look at various aspects of Calvin's life and work that throw particular light on him as a pastor.[5] We will examine his theology, character, suffering and missionary zeal, but first a little background.

On the evening of a day in July, 1536, a carriage from France arrived in Geneva, Switzerland. It held, amongst others, John Calvin, his brother Anthony and their sister. Like many other French Protestants, they had fled from France because of Roman Catholic persecution. The exigencies of the war between Francis I and Charles V—or perhaps, more accurately, the providence of God—forced them to travel via Geneva en route to Basel where they hoped to stay for some time.

In Geneva the Protestant Reformation was being led by Froment, Viret and William Farel. The latter was a colourful extrovert from Auvergne. A man of tempestuous nature, he had stormed Geneva with the Gospel, winning many to its cause. Farel, however, was wise enough to recognise his own limitations and knew that in time Geneva would need an abler man to grasp the reins if Biblical reformation was to be properly worked out. Upon hearing that Calvin had arrived in Geneva from France, he went posthaste to see him at The Bear's Inn. After a long altercation in which Farel threatened to call down God's judgement upon him, Calvin agreed to remain and enter into the reformation work in Geneva.

On Farel's recommendation the Genevan City Council appointed Calvin as Reader in Theology or Reader in the Holy Scriptures. This allowed him to preach in St. Peter's. Of so little importance was this to the Council that in their minutes of September 5, 1536, they refer to Calvin as "ille Gallus"—this man from Gaule (France).

It was only towards the close of 1536 that he received a pastoral office, at first as Farel's assistant. Thus Calvin entered into his long association with the Church in Geneva. We must never forget that within the city of Geneva, and in his own view of his work, Calvin was in many ways pre-eminently a pastor of a church, not merely a theologian or academic figure or even an international reformer. For some 25 years, excluding his three years of exile, he was engaged in preaching, counselling, writing, struggling, suffering, planning and evangelising—as a pastor!

1. *The Pastor's Theology*

James Denney said on one occasion: "Every theologian should be an evangelist and every evangelist should be a theologian". It is equally true that every pastor should be a theologian and every theologian a pastor![6] John Calvin was an excellent demonstrator of this truth. His example provides a complete refutation of much current evangelical thinking, which separates these two facets and almost makes them mutually exclusive.

Calvin's theology was never conceived or practised in a sterile vacuum; what he believed, he practised. Indeed it was because of his theological views that he took his pastoral office so seriously. We may go further and say that his doctrinal views enabled him to function as a Biblical pastor should. Let me elaborate briefly on Calvin's theology, with particular reference to his doctrine of the church.

In striking contrast to today's Evangelicalism, Calvin and the other Reformers thought of God's dealings with his children, almost exclusively in terms of the framework of the Church, be it Catholic (universal) or local. Thus, Calvin points out, God met his people in the Old Testament period *in* the Tabernacle or *in* the Temple, and through the ministry of the Levites. In the New Testament this truth continues in the invisible church, visibly manifested. The church is our mother from which we are born and by whom we are nourished. Moreover, through the faithful preaching of the Word and dispensing of the sacraments (by those duly called to this task), the Christian experiences forgiveness, grace and sanctification. He has now become a definite member of a definite family—the family of God—and his life is incomplete if he ignores it or circulates outside it.

71

For a church to be true there have to be the distinguishing marks of preaching of the Word, the dispensing of the sacraments and discipline. I should add by way of enlargement that in Calvin's understanding of the New Testament, the pastor is also a preacher! He would have denied strongly the modern dichotomy between these two functions.[7] He himself preached well over 250 times a year. Indeed, there is evidence that it may have been considerably more, for he speaks of preaching "every day". Furthermore there must be a subordination to the church, for as he says: ". . . no man may with impunity spurn her authority, or reject her admonitions, or resist her counsels, or make sport of her censures, far less revolt from her, and violate her unity . . . So highly does he recommend her authority, that when it is violated he considers that his own authority is impaired".[8] Again, to be a true church, there must be a Biblical Church order. Thus, in his now famous *Church Constitution* which he presented to the city-government of Geneva, he laid down from Scripture the necessity of having preachers, doctors, elders and deacons. Finally, we must mention that while the church is not yet perfect, nevertheless she should jealously guard her purity. In other words, the admission or exclusion of individuals from the Lord's Table is not to be a haphazard procedure, but an active concern, whereby the church seeks to keep herself pure.

In all this (and, we add, in every other department of Christian Doctrine) Calvin always stressed, (i) The glory of God and his Son. To defy or defile the church of God was to dishonour the Lord of the church. (ii) The spiritual welfare of the church. Of Calvin's 4,271 letters preserved a large number are addressed to churches.

This very brief theological survey is absolutely crucial for an understanding of much of Calvin's conflict and suffering as a pastor. It was precisely his Biblical and doctrinal views of God's church and the pastoral office which drove him to act so vigorously as the Pastor of Geneva's growing Protestant church, and which brought him into conflict with the government of Geneva. An application to today's Evangelical church lies readily at hand; we need to grasp afresh the truth that no man can ever function as an adequate pastor unless he works within a framework of scriptural doctrine, and in particular within the framework of the doctrine of the Church.

2. *The Pastor's Character*

Nobody doubts that Calvin had weaknesses. Nevertheless, there is enough evidence to suggest that contrary to popular opinion, he did exemplify the instructions of Paul to Timothy in 2 Timothy 2:24, "And the servant of the Lord must not strive; but be gentle unto all men, apt to teach, patient; In meekness instructing those that oppose themselves; if God peradventure will give them repentance to the acknowledging of the truth".

Calvin had a shy, retiring nature, perhaps even being something of an introvert. In his altercation with Farel, when the latter was seeking to batter down his excuses for not remaining in Geneva, Calvin's sensitive nature was revealed in the sheer terror with which he heard Farel threaten to pronounce God's judgement upon him. One of the arguments he used in an attempt to fend off Farel he put this way: "I am timid, weak, and fainthearted by nature, and feel myself not equal to such opposition".[9]

In the heated and bitter controversy over the Lord's Supper, which set the Lutherans and the Zwinglians at each other's throats, Calvin sought (if we may change the metaphor) to pour oil on troubled waters. His aim in writing his work *Brief Treatise on the Holy Lord's Supper* was primarily to bring about concord amongst the different evangelical communions. A contemporary vividly describes how Luther, having ended a lecture and being surrounded by students, entered the bookshop of the Wittenberger Moritz Goltsch. Upon asking what new books Goltsch had purchased at the Frankfurt Fair he was given Calvin's short work on the Lord's Supper. He immediately sat down and read it and when he had completed it confessed in deep contemplation that if Zwingli and Oekolampad ". . . had so declared themselves from the start, we would never have been involved in so lengthy a controversy".[10]

Again, we see the graciousness in his attitude to two of the pastors who remained in Geneva during his exile and allowed themselves to become pawns of the anti-Reformation party. Upon his return he could no doubt have insisted upon their removal, or at least made life unpleasant for them. He did neither, but showed patience and longsuffering.

This attitude became particularly apparent in his pastoral work in the Genevan church. He robbed himself of sleep. His home was always open to anyone seeking advice. He was constantly in touch with all the affairs of the church and state. He visited the sick and lackadaisical, and knew almost every citizen; all in the midst of continuing illness, writing, heavy commitments in preaching and lecturing and attention to the minutiae that crowd every pastor's life.

Not only was his home open to give any advice that Genevans might seek, but he showed constant hospitality in providing lodgings for strangers passing through the city. This, by the way, was one reason why he received a higher remuneration than his colleagues. Incessant labours crowded his hours. What pastor does not sympathise with his lament, in January, 1542 (he returned to Geneva from exile in September, 1541): "Since my arrival here I can only remember having been granted two hours in which no one has come and disturbed me"?[11] Thus was Calvin's theology forged and applied in the daily, yea, hourly furnace of intense pastoral work, counselling and practical decision making! Here was no ivory-tower theologian!

He also took his turn in the normal duties expected of the other pastors in Geneva, namely preaching, lecturing, baptising and visiting. He never dispensed with routine work allotted to him because of any superior eminence of position. Even when he approached death he did not stay away from the regular pastors' meetings where they practised what was called "grabeau", or mutual criticism. He willingly and humbly took his fair share of pastoral criticism from his colleagues.

In the terrible plague which visited Geneva in 1543 Calvin wrote to a friend in Lausanne: "I fear that if something happens to Blanchet it will be up to me to take his place. For we belong to every member of our flock and cannot withdraw ourselves from those who most need our assistance".[12] This quotation clearly underlines the direct relationship between Calvin's theology and his practice. His desire to come to the aid of the plague victims springs directly from his grasp of the fact that they belonged to the Flock of God. Once again we see how his doctrine of the Church governed his pastoral actions within the church. It was only the Council's persistent refusal which frustrated his determination to carry his theology into practice when at last Blanchet did become a plague victim.

3. *The Pastor's Suffering*

In John 5:18-21 our Lord warned his disciples that they would suffer as his servants, just as he did and on his behalf: "A servant is not greater than his Lord".

To begin with, there was a time when Calvin had to suffer the traditional pastoral affliction of financial poverty. After Farel had introduced him to the city Council and they had cryptically recorded their interview with "that Frenchman" it took another five months before they decided to give him any remuneration! They agreed to pay him five Sonnentaler, and this was after he had already been in their employ for that period. How many modern pastors would wait five months for their first stipend cheque?

His years of exile in Strasbourg did not improve matters. He was so poor at one stage that he had to sell his household utensils and even his beloved library. Any book-loving pastor will know what that involves! Only after eight months in Strasbourg, and after he had been in their employ for almost that whole period, did he receive a salary for his lectures of a Gulden a week. A few weeks before his death, in Geneva in 1564, the city Council (they had travelled far from those early years) made him a gift of money and sent it through his brother, but although Calvin had suffered poverty, the wealth of this world had no attraction for him and he refused it, like he had refused other, earlier gifts.

However, this suffering was small in comparison with what he suffered for the sake of the Church and the Christian Gospel. At the height of his conflict with the Libertine party, the city Council records disclose all kinds of subversive attempts by his enemies to discredit him. "Even love letters without name or date were smuggled to him to undermine his reputation." [13]

For many years, until the Reformation became established, he could not walk across a street without being mocked, his name twisted to "Cain"; more than one dog was named after him, and on many occasions his life was in mortal danger. The Libertines, on one occasion, drew swords in St. Peter's and on another Calvin himself counted between 50 and 60 arquebuss shots fired outside the door of his house.

On top of this Calvin had to cope with constant, racking illnesses. O. R. Johnston lists them as follows: "From about the age of thirty we are told that he suffered from headaches, catarrh, asthma and indigestion. On occasions he could not see his lecture notes because his vision was so impaired by migraine. After 1558, when he had an attack of quartan fever, he was never anything but an invalid, stricken with arthritis, haemorrhoids and the pleurisy leading to tuberculosis. He was ceaselessly in pain, and had finally to be carried to the cathedral to preach".[14] To these Stickelberger adds the following: "Subjected to maladies of the trachea, he had with pains in his side to spit blood when he had used his voice too much in the pulpit. Several attacks of pleurisy prepared the way for consumption whose helpless victim he became at the age of fifty-one . . . He was plagued by gallstones and kidney stones in addition to stomach cramps and wicked intestinal influenzas . . . It was no exaggeration when he parenthetically wrote in a letter, 'If only my condition were not a constant death struggle . . .'." [15]

While his marriage to Idellete de Buren was a happy one, the couple lost three children at birth, no small sorrow in itself! Some years later one of his adversaries reproached him for the fact that he had no children, to which Calvin replied: "My sons are to be found all over the world".[16]

Saddest of all were the moral and doctrinal failures of friends, intimates, colleagues and relatives. Who does not know this experience! Among them was Sebastian Castellio, who was the Rector of Calvin's new college in Geneva. Brilliant as an educationalist and ahead of his time in matters relating to the freedom of the conscience, he was nevertheless ambitious, quarrelsome and impulsive. He threw away a magnificent opportunity when he espoused some liberal views. Calvin drank deeply of the cup of suffering when the wife of his brother Anthony was caught committing adultery in Calvin's own home with his factotum Peter Daguet. The court proceedings further revealed that this trusted man had been stealing from Calvin for years. Anthony finally divorced her. To Calvin this would bring the further blight and scandal of divorce right into his own home. One can well imagine what sport the anti-Reformation party must have had with this sad event.

There was still more to follow: the Reformer's own stepchild, Judith, the daughter of Idellette de Buren, fell into the same sin of immorality. So crushed was Calvin that he had to leave Geneva for a few days' rest in the country, something he never did even at the height of other conflicts.

4. *The Pastor as missionary and evangelist*

Calvin's love for the Church and for the souls of men was basic in the establishment of his Academy or College in 1559. Under his training, over 100 men went out as pastors, missionaries, evangelists or colporteurs between 1555 and 1562. Their geographical range of activity indicates Calvin's genuine concern for God's work everywhere for we find them going to France, the Piedmont Valleys, Turin, Antwerp, London and even Brazil. Already in Strasbourg, while in exile from Geneva, Calvin trained a few students for the ministry. In the same year, 1540, in a letter to Beza, he indicated his deep desire for pastors who would continue in that work. The very opening sentence shows again his love and concern for the Church: "If we would really make provision for the profit of the Church, we must call to the office of pastor people who will be able some day to take on the responsibility after us".[17]   Note again how church-centred and pastor-centred Calvin was in his thinking. The possibility of Christian service outside the visible manifestation of the Church in its local form never crossed his mind!

Together with this growing educational institution, Geneva became famous for her printing trade, for many refugees had fled to her for refuge bringing with them their skills. Thus Geneva poured forth Bibles, Catechisms, Hymn Books, Theological works, Commentaries and general Christian literature. These flowed out across Europe in an ever increasing stream. Again we see the Biblical emphasis on the local church and its importance, for the church in Geneva became a fountainhead of missionary and evangelistic endeavour. Calvin's great desire was to spread the Gospel, and that Gospel he succintly summarises in his Institutes when he says: "Therefore, the moment we turn aside from him (Christ) in the minutest degree, salvation, which resides entirely in him, gradually disappears; so that all who do not rest in him voluntarily deprive themselves of all grace".[18]

It is also satisfying to discover that Calvin had no small part in the establishment of French Reformed Churches which in 1555 numbered exactly one, namely the church in Paris, and in 1561 (a mere six years later) numbered 2,150 churches![19] Many of the pastors of these churches were trained in Geneva and many who were converted and joined these churches were thus only the end result of Calvin's own pastoral ministry and desire to spread the Gospel as widely as possible.

Indeed, it is even more thrilling to discover that Cadier himself bears testimony to the power of Calvin's written ministry by referring to a man he knew who came to a saving faith in Christ through reading the Institutes![20] Thus does the great evangelistic thrust begun in Geneva's church, printing and publishing houses still continue to this day.

Conclusions

We have thought of Calvin in relation to his theology, his character, his suffering and his missionary concern.

Beginning with the first of these we recall that lying at the foundation of all the God wrought through him was an outstanding grasp of theology, a theology which has given strength and backbone to countless churches since that time. The effect and benefit of Calvin's books and commentaries, which continue to be in demand by all those who esteem thorough exposition of the Scriptures is beyond calculation. Ours is an age of appalling spiritual weakness in which theology is treated with impatience. Spiritual experience is given first place whereas true experience should follow the enlightenment which truth brings. Little wonder, then, that so much activity in the churches is characterised by superficiality. Our generation is infantile because theological perception is dim. John Calvin reminds us that theology, doctrine and faith are primary and not secondary needs.

Not disconnected to theology is character. Character is strengthened by faith. Although averse by nature to conflict and controversy Calvin never gave up. He did not forsake his post despite constant pain and illness.

Is this not a rebuke to ministers who, with only a fraction of tribulation, are ready to quit, or look for an easier position?

With such pressure of work the Genevan reformer could well have confined his efforts to Switzerland but his vision for reformation extended to all people and to future generations. His missionary zeal was not circumscribed. True, he did not think, as we do today, in terms of reaching every language group but then the world was not open in the sense that it is today. The lesson, surely, is that he did his utmost where the door of opportunity opened to him. We do well to follow his example.

REFERENCES

[1] Emmanuel Stickelberger, *Calvin,* James Clarke, London, 1959, p. 53.

[2] Jean Cadier, *The Man God Mastered,* Inter-Varsity Fellowship, London, 1960, p. 22.

[3] A. H. Newman, *A Manual of Church History,* Vol. II, The American Baptist Publication Society, Philadelphia, 1957, pp. 216-217.

[4] H. Daniel-Rops, *History of the Church of Christ,* Vol. IV, The Protestant Reformation, J. M. Dent and Sons, London, 1963, pp. 415-417.

[5] I am using the word "Pastor" to include the office of Preaching and Ruling Elder, and therefore recognise that a man may be an Elder and so apt to teach, but not necessarily given to public preaching.

[6] It is, surely, significant that with monotonous regularity the leading modern theologians move out of pastoral circles into what really are no more than academic ivory-castles. By contrast the Puritans, and probably the majority of Scottish, Welsh, English and American Evangelical leaders in the 17th, 18th and even the 19th Centuries, were both pastors and theologians. Jonathan Edwards is perhaps the most notable example.

[7] This is not to deny that amongst elders some do not have a direct public preaching ministry, although they must all be "apt to teach" (1 Tim. 3:2).

[8] John Calvin, *Institutes of the Christian Religion*, James Clarke, London, 1957, Book IV, I, 10, p. 290.

[9] Calvin, *Commentaire sur le Livre de Psaumes*, 1859, p. IX, quoted Stickelberger, op. cit., p. 47.

[10] Paul Henry, *Das Leben Johannes Calvins*, Hamburg, 1838, Vol. II, pp. 502 f., quoted Stickelberger, op. cit., p. 68.

[11] Cadier, op. cit., p. 119.

[12] Rudolf Schwarz, *Johannes Calvins Lebenswerk in seinen Briefen*, Tuebingen, 1909, Vol. I, p. 160, quoted by Stickelberger, op. cit., p. 97.

[13] Stickelberger, op. cit., p. 134.

[14] O. R. Johnston, *Calvin the Man*, paper read at the Puritan and Reformed Studies Conference, December, 1964, quoted from Conference papers entitled "Able Ministers of The New Testament", p. 27.

[15] Stickelberger, op. cit., p. 86. [16] Cadier, op. cit., p. 101. [17] Cadier, op. cit., p. 136.

[18] John Calvin, *Institutes of the Christian Religion*, James Clarke, London, 1957.

[19] Cadier, op. cit., p. 167 states that these figures were given to Catherine de Medici, by Admiral Coligny. Cadier's phrasing suggests that we must treat these figures with caution, but even halving them is indicative of enormous growth.

[20] Cadier, op. cit., p. 178.

Church Discipline among the Anabaptists

David Kingdon

I MUST BEGIN BY STATING THE LIMITS OF OUR CONSIDERATION. I INTEND TO confine myself to a study of the evangelical, or biblicist Anabaptists, not because the revolutionary Anabaptists or the contemplative Anabaptists are unimportant, but because our theological sympathies are obviously with the evangelical Anabaptists. In saying this, however, I do not wish to attempt a judgment on the vexed issue of the extent, if any, of Anabaptist influence on Baptist origins.

I propose to divide the subject into the following sections:

i The historical context in which Anabaptist ideas on church discipline arose.

ii The theological principles involved in the Anabaptist understanding of church discipline.

iii The exercise of church discipline.

iv Issues arising from the exercise of church discipline.

v The relevance of Anabaptist thinking for our own day.

i The Historical Context

G. H. Williams has emphasised the importance of this in relation to believers' churches in general, and the Anabaptists in particular. He writes: "In the sixteenth century the Anabaptist conventicles, unfolding in their astoundingly mobile and martyr-minded vitality represent a spiritual growth inexplicable apart from the previous generation with its disciplines and despairs."[1] Even though the Anabaptists sought to restore the primitive church *de novo*, they could not escape the conditioning of history. Thus, although the Anabaptists did challenge the sacralist concept of the Church which the Reformers carried over, largely uncritically, from medieval Christendom, it is also right to appreciate the fact that they themselves may well have been influenced by medieval sects such as the Waldensians, though of course the extent of such influence is still a matter for debate.[2]

If the extent of the influence of medieval sects is not yet determined, what is clear is that Anabaptist ideas on church discipline were largely worked out in antithesis to the teaching and practice of the Magisterial Reformation, as G. H. Williams terms the Lutheran and Calvinist sections of the Reformation movement. Basic to the Magisterial Reformation is the conviction that the instrument of the reform of the Church should be the civic power, whether the "godly prince" as in Luther's Germany or the city council as in Calvin's Geneva. As an ideal, the reform of the Church by means of the power of the state was upheld even when the Reformation movement represented a small minority in a predominantly Catholic country.

Intimately related to this ideal is a territorial view of the Church as embracing all the citizens of an area or country by virtue of their (infant) baptism. When, in 1531, Melanchthon drew up a memorandum on Anabaptism in which the death penalty was prescribed for Anabaptists, it is this territorial conception of the Church which is in the foreground. "What would happen," he asks, "if children were not baptised, if not that our whole society would become openly heathen?. . . it is a serious matter to cast children out of Christendom and to have two sets of people, the one baptised and the other unbaptised. . ."[3] In complete agreement with the identification of Christian discipleship with citizenship is the Zurich reformer, Ulrich Zwingli: "The Christian is none other than the good and faithful citizen, and the Christian city none other than a Christian church."[4]

The Anabaptists completely rejected the territorial conception of the Church. To their mind the Church was a covenantal community of converted men and women who were pledged and active disciples of Christ. For them Church and State were not two sides of the same coin but two distinct spheres. Their view was that the Church was separated from the world through the action of God in regenerating a people for the praise of his name. As Menno Simons put it: "The entire evangelical Scriptures teach us that the Church of Christ was and is, in doctrine, life and worship, a people separated from the world".[5]

Most modern scholars locate the emergence of the evangelical Baptist movement at Zurich during the years 1524-1525. The leaders of the movement were former supporters of Ulrich Zwingli, who not only disagreed with his policy of gradual reform but desired the restoration of the primitive, apostolic church composed of visible saints. As they searched Scripture, and especially the New Testament, they became convinced that only the baptism of professed believers was sanctioned by its teaching.

The decisive break between the "Brethren", as they preferred to be known, and Zwingli came when the city council decreed in January 1525 that all who failed to have their infants baptised within eight days would be exiled. On January 21, 1525, three days after the issuing of the decree, four leaders of the Brethren were expelled from Zurich, and two others who were citizens, Conrad Grebel and Felix Manz, were forbidden to hold any more "schools" for agitation. That same day, in the evening, Grebel baptised George Blaurock, a former priest, by affusion (pouring), on profession of his faith. Blaurock then baptised his companions. The account of this historic meeting in the *Hutterite Chronicle* says, very movingly, "Thus they together gave themselves to the name of the Lord in the high fear of God. Each confirmed the other in the service of the Gospel and began to teach and keep the faith. Therewith began the separation from the world and its evil works."[6]

Though it was chiefly in contrast to the teaching of the Magisterial Reformation that the evangelical Anabaptists worked out, through a careful study of Scripture, their principles of church discipline, they were very well aware that the battle had to be fought on another front as well.

The Anabaptist movement had not been in existence ten years before the disastrous episode of Munster (1533-1536) and a similar one at Amsterdam, brought unjustified abuse upon the whole Anabaptist community. Unhinged fanatics, stirred up by apocalyptic expectations, presumed to anticipate the Second Coming by setting up a Christian commonwealth at Munster, which they saw as the location of the New Jerusalem. Soon polygamy appeared, and sins punishable by death included blasphemy, seditious language, scolding one's parents, back-biting, spreading scandal and complaining.

Most remarkably, it was the Munster episode and its immediate aftermath which brought into the ranks of the Anabaptists a priest of the Church of Rome who was to become the outstanding leader of the scattered communities of the Brethren.

Menno Simons, who was born in 1496, at Witmarsum in the province of Friesland, became a priest in 1525, the same year that the evangelical Anabaptists of Zurich founded their church. Within a short while after his ordination Menno began to have doubts about the Catholic dogma of transubstantiation. Through a study of the New Testament he became convinced that Roman teaching on the mass was false, but he remained in

F

the Catholic Church for he was not prepared hastily to leave a good position and a generous income. Gradually he began to question the practice of infant baptism, but he was not forced to think seriously about it until 1531, when on March 20 a tailor by the name of Sicke Freeks was publicly executed in the neighbouring city of Leeuwarden for the crime of being baptised a second time. Menno was amazed that a pious, godly man, as he learned that Freeks was, should have been prepared to die for the sake of a "second baptism". Was it possible that Menno's church was as wrong about baptism as he had discovered it to be about the mass?

Again Menno searched the Scripture, and again he found that it did not sanction either Rome's teaching or practice. Turning to his superior at Pingjuin for help he found none. Nor were his evangelical contemporaries, the reformers, able to guide him, for they all taught that infants should be baptised, though for differing reasons. So Menno concluded that "all were deceived about infant baptism", and that baptism on confession of faith alone was scriptural.

Yet still Menno lingered, Lot-like, in the Church of Rome. In 1534 a division occurred in his parish when certain persons of the "sect of Munster" reached Witmarsum, and "deceived many pious hearts in our village". For over a year Menno fought the effects of Munsterite fanaticism on the more pious members of his flock. His own brother was swept away by it, to Menno's great distress. So vigorous was Menno in his public denunciation of the Munsterites that he won the reputation of being able "to stop the mouths of the enemy very well".

Menno finally decided to carry the battle against the Munsterites still further by attacking their beliefs in writing. Early in 1535 he wrote a little pamphlet entitled *A Clear and Indubitable Proof from Holy Scripture Against the Abominable and Great Blasphemy of Jan van Leiden*. It was not printed until 1627.

However, another conflict arose in Menno's mind. By attacking the Munsterites and not offering anything better, was he not encouraging pious souls to think he was merely a defender of the Roman Church? The climax to Menno's conflict came when three hundred souls stirred up by Munsterite errors decided to set up their own new Jerusalem in Friesland. In March 1535 they seized an old monastery (Oude Kloster) outside the city of Bolsward and entrenched themselves against attack. The forces of the government laid siege, and after 130 Munsterites had been killed the remainder were captured and executed on April 7. Among them was Menno's own brother.

This terrible event made an impression upon Menno which he could not shake off. If they could give their blood for a false faith, why was he not prepared to give anything for the truth? He felt that their blood lay upon his soul. "The blood of these people," he said, "became such a burden to me that I could not endure it nor find rest in my soul".

By the strange workings of Providence, Menno had been brought to the parting of the ways. The path of duty became clear. He could no longer evade his responsibility of caring for the erring sheep. In deep agony of soul Menno turned to God. "My heart trembled in my body," he recalls. "I prayed God with sighs and tears that he would give me, a troubled sinner, the gift of his grace and create a clean heart in me, that through the merits of the crimson blood of Christ he would graciously forgive my unclean walk and ease-seeking life, and bestow upon me wisdom, candour, and courage, that I might preach his exalted and adorable name and Holy Word unadulterated and make manifest his truth to his praise."

For nine months he publicly declared from his pulpit in Witmarsum the necessity of repentance and faith, believers' baptism and the proper understanding of the Lord's Supper. Probably on Sunday, January 30, 1536, he voluntarily resigned his charge and renounced his priesthood to embark upon a life of danger, ministering to the scattered flocks of Anabaptist believers in the Northern Netherlands and North-West Germany until he died on January 31, 1561.[7]

I have spent some time on the early life of Menno Simons because it illustrates the point that Anabaptist writers on church discipline had to fight on two fronts. On the one hand they felt obliged to set right the views of the Reformers, who in their view were still maintaining a Romish doctrine of the Church. On the other, they did battle with the fanaticism of the Munsterites and others who sought to exalt the Holy Spirit at the expense of the written word of Scripture. If I am not mistaken, our task as Reformed Baptists is not much different today. The heirs of the Reformers, so far as their doctrine of the Church is concerned, are still with us, and if the extremism of the men of Munster is happily no longer in evidence, their leading principle still is, breaking out in those who in our day attempt to magnify the Spirit by belittling the Word of God written by the Spirit.

ii The Theological Principles

The evangelical Anabaptists might be described as Bible-searchers. Eager to know the truth of God, they gave themselves unstintingly to the study of Scripture. They were well aware of the importance of what they were doing. As Balthasar Hubmaier put it in the *Eighteen Dissertations:* "It is an old custom that comes to us from the times of the Apostles, that when evil things befall concerning the faith, all men who wish to speak the word of God, and are of a Christian way of thinking, should assemble to search the Scriptures."[8]

As they searched the Scriptures, they came to an understanding of discipleship and of the nature of the Church which marked them off from the Magisterial Reformers to whom they were ready to acknowledge their indebtedness in other matters.

Harold S. Bender has argued, I believe convincingly, that, "First and fundamental in the Anabaptist vision was the conception of the essence of Christianity as discipleship".[9] Reacting against the Lutheran *sola fideism* (faith alone), which so often did not appear to issue in transformation of life, the Anabaptists insisted that regeneration is evidenced by newness of life. Pilgram Marpeck, a leader of the South German Anabaptists, is representative of many who joined the Anabaptists because the libertinism of the Lutheran Reformation profoundly disappointed him.[10] Constantly as we read about these men we are made aware that, for the evangelical Anabaptists, the true test of the Christian is discipleship. For them the great word is not so much "faith" as "following". Not that they would deny the importance of faith, but they were concerned that it should not be isolated from discipleship. Thus Menno, with the churches of the Magisterial Reformation very much in mind, avers that, "before God no outward baptism counts, nor staying away from the churches, nor Lord's Supper, nor persecution, if there is no obedience to the commands of God, and no faith which manifests itself in love, and no new creature".[11] Active, obedient, loving discipleship which embraces all aspects of human conduct and shows itself in every human relationship is Menno's great concern as a writer. He says that "it profits nothing to move about in the inward communion of the brethren if we are not inwardly in the communion of our beloved Lord Jesus Christ",[12] and for him union with Christ is evidenced by the imitation of Christ.

That the evangelical Anabaptists lived out their teaching, even their enemies had to admit. Typical is this grudging admission from Heinrich Bullinger, one of their bitterest opponents: "Those who unite with them will by their ministers be received into their church by rebaptism and repentance and newness of life. They henceforth lead their lives under a semblance of a quite spiritual conduct. They denounce covetousness, pride, profanity, the lewd conversation and immorality of the world, drinking and gluttony. In short, their hypocrisy is great and manifold."[13]

Baptism, according to Anabaptist teaching, introduced these baptised to both the life of discipleship and the discipline of the covenanted community, the church. For them it was the "covenant of a good conscience toward God". (1 Peter 3:21.) Here they followed Luther's translation which calls baptism the "Bund eines guten Gewissens mit Gott".[14] (Good conscience with God.) They viewed baptism less as the symbol of a past experience and more as the pledge of a complete, present and continuing commitment to obey Christ.[15] This commitment was understood as having implications for the person baptised, not only as an individual, but also in his relationship to the believing community to which baptism introduced him. This is made clear in the following quotation, probably from Hans Hut:[16] "One receives the sign of baptism as a covenant (bund) of dedication (verwilligung) before a Christian church which itself received the covenant from God in his name and has the power and authority to share it with all those who have a heartfelt desire for it. As the Lord said, 'what you shall bind on earth shall also be bound in heaven. . .' This covenant is a dedication to the obedience of Christ with a rendering of divine love toward all the brethren and sisters with body, life, goods, and honour, irrespective of what evil the world may say to him."[17]

From the Anabaptist conception of discipleship there follows, secondly, a new concept of the Church. "Voluntary church membership based upon true conversion and involving a commitment to holy living and discipleship was the absolutely essential heart of this concept." Obviously such a Church had to be regarded as distinct and separate from the state. Being thus separated in their own Christian society, the Anabaptists expected the hatred and opposition of the world.

The Church was thought of not only as a separated people, but positively it was regarded as a brotherhood. The Anabaptists did more than pay lip-service to this ideal. They worked it out in the practicalities of life, taking the voluntary sharing of goods in the primitive church at Jerusalem as their model. In some Anabaptist communities voluntary communism of goods became the way of life. In 1528 the Hutterite Brotherhood adopted Christian communism, and have continued to practise it to the present day. Other groups did not go this far, but they emphasised that the Christian is only a steward of his property, which love will make available to meet a brother's needs. Harold Bender cites the testimony of a Protestant visitor to a Swiss Brethren baptismal service held in Strasbourg in 1557.[18] He reported that a question addressed to all applicants for baptism was: "Whether they, if necessity require it, would devote all their possessions to the service of the brotherhood, and would not fail any member that is in need, if they were able to render aid."[19]

In conceiving of the church as a brotherhood, the Anabaptists stressed the importance of each member watching over not only his own soul, but, in brotherly love, the souls of his fellow believers. In this connection, they placed great emphasis upon the disciplinary process outlined in Matthew 18:15-18. Once again, baptism was connected in Anabaptist thinking with what they termed, referring to the text in Matthew, as "fraternal discipline". In Balthasar Hubmaier's Baptismal Order, as followed at Nicolsburg, the candidate is asked by the presiding elder, "If thou hereafter sinnest and they brother knoweth it, wilt thou accept from him the first and the second steps of fraternal discipline, and then, if necessary, willingly and obediently allow thyself to be disciplined before the church?"[20] Baptism, then, commits one not only to a life of discipleship but also to the discipline of the brotherhood. Thus, the church is not the optional extra which it is for many evangelical Christians today, rather it is "a brotherhood of love in which the fulness of the Christian life ideal is to be expressed".[21]

The third great element in the Anabaptist vision was the ethic of love and non-resistance as applied to every area of life in society. The Anabaptist might carry a staff, but never a sword, for he renounced warfare, strife and violence. Yet he was not naively pacifistic, for outside of "the perfection of Christ" there was still needed the state to maintain law and order by using, if necessary, the sword. For the Anabaptists to be under the New Covenant meant that the taking of human life was not permissible. As Conrad Grebel wrote: "True Christians use neither worldly sword nor engage in war, since among them taking human life has ceased entirely, for we are no longer under the Old Covenant. . . The Gospel and those who accept it are not to be protected with the sword, neither should they thus protect themselves."[22]

So far as church discipline was concerned, this understanding of the demands of the ethic of love defined both the body which exercised discipline and the ultimate sanction which could be applied when discipline had to be carried out by the church. Not the magistrate, as in the Lutheran and Calvinist Reformations, but the brotherhood was responsible for discipline. The sphere of the magistrate lay altogether outside of "the perfection of Christ". The final decision lay neither with the godly prince nor with the city council but with the whole congregation.

The ultimate sanction was not the death penalty, as it was in Luther's Germany and Calvin's Geneva, but the ban, which was held to have replaced the death penalty prescribed in the Old Testament for certain offences.

The introduction of the ban had been one of the principal demands of the Brethren at Zurich, but after a period of wavering Zwingli rejected it on the ground that the punishment of blasphemers by the government made the ban unnecessary.[23]

By their insistence that discipline should be exercised by the brotherhood, the Anabaptists challenged the fatal confusion of sacralism which had for centuries failed to see that punitive measures in society must never be intermingled with punitive measures in the church. The sacralist confusion finds its classic expression in Thomas Aquinas who taught that heresy is a thing for which a man deserves "not only to be separated from the Church by excommunication but also barred from the world by death".[24] As Verduin points out, it comes as a shock to realise that discipline as one of the marks of the Church was not only absent from the Reformer's earliest delineation of the Church, but was actually opposed as a piece of Anabaptist fanaticism. Calvin, for example, argued against the Anabaptist case for discipline at the Lord's table by saying that 1 Corinthians 5:11 "has to do with private association and not at all with the public communion. If the Church puts up with an unworthy person then let him who knows it keep himself from the man in his private contacts. . . but he is not to make a schism nor separation in regard to the public communion".[25] In other words, it is permissible to sit with a rogue or knave at the Lord's table but right to avoid him at all other times! As late as 1552 a Reformed opponent of Menno Simons was arguing that "the papistical abomination by its abuse has so frightfully destroyed the ordinance of the churches and the right use of the ban, that it cannot be re-established suddenly".[26]

In fairness to the Reformers, however, it must be pointed out that, having opted for reformation by means of the civil power, they created a problem for themselves when they sought to re-introduce church discipline. The evangelical magistrates having been liberated from the yoke of papal domination did not prove at all keen on submitting themselves, and the higher echelons of society, to ecclesiastical discipline exercised by the leaders of the church. The story of Calvin's struggle with the city council of Geneva over the issue of discipline is a classic illustration of the dilemma which faced the Reformers when they attempted to re-introduce church discipline.

The Anabaptists, of course, faced no such dilemma. Rejecting sacralism root and branch they denied to the magistrate any place whatever in the affairs of the church. For them, church discipline was to be exercised by the brotherhood and not by the government.

iii The Exercise of Church Discipline

As I have already remarked, baptism served, in Anabaptist thinking, to link the believer with the brotherhood, pledging him not only to walk in newness of life but also to live in community with the brethren. In this respect they recovered the New Testament view of discipleship as a commitment to Christ and to the Church, his body (see *e.g.* Rom. 2:1-13).

Before the Reformers did so explicitly, the Anabaptists taught that discipline is one of the marks of the true church of Christ. Menno Simons speaks for all evangelical Anabaptists when he writes: "For as a city without walls and gates, or a field without trenches and fences, and a house without walls and doors, so also is a church which has not the true apostolic exclusion or ban."[27]

Firstly, we shall consider the necessity for church discipline. Menno regarded church discipline as necessary because the Scriptures require it. The key texts are Matthew 18:15-18; John 20:23; 1 Corinthians 5:11; 1 Timothy 5:20 and Galatians 6:1. The fact that Christ commanded it and the apostolic church practised it was sufficient reason for its re-introduction in the restored church of the New Testament which the Anabaptists sought to establish. It was, in Menno's words, the "express ordinance of Christ and his holy apostles".[28]

Again, church discipline is necessary in order that the church of Christ might be kept pure. The Church is the bride of Christ, pledged to have none other but Christ as her husband. Without discipline, the separation of the church from the world would become blurred and indistinct. To use Menno's vivid metaphor, the church would become like a city without

87

walls, a prey to its enemies who would come in like a flood and destroy its life. Church discipline is needed, then, as a rampart against sin and error. More positively, through "fraternal admonition" the members of the church encourage each other to advance in holiness, following in the way of Christ.

If the necessity of church discipline resides in the fact that Christ commands it and the life of the church demands it, there was also a pressing contemporary reason for its practice in the churches of the evangelical Anabaptists Only by the maintenance of a proper discipline could their churches be freed of the reproach of Munster. Menno spells out the contemporary challenge: "It is more than evident that if we had not been zealous in this matter in these days, we would be considered and called by every man the companions of the sect of Munster and all perverted sects."[29]

Secondly, the Anabaptists viewed church discipline as brotherly, or fraternal, discipline which is to be exercised in love. "If your *brother* sins. . ." (Matt. 18:15) was taken seriously with equal emphasis being placed upon the fact of brotherhood as upon his sin. The fact that he is a brother places him under obligation to receive fraternal admonition and, what is often forgotten, the wronged brother under a loving obligation to exercise it. By emphasising the nature of the church as a brotherhood, Anabaptist writers linked the initial process of discipling (evangelism) with the continuing process of discipling (sanctification). Thus, they took a much more positive view of discipline than the word conjures up in our minds today. For them, discipline was not the last resort of the church against an erring brother, but the continuing expression of brotherly love. Even the ban (or excommunication) was brought under this rule. As Menno puts it: "the ban is a great work of love, notwithstanding it is looked upon by the foolish as an act of great hatred."[30] Provided such a view of church discipline is maintained, it is freed from the two dangers of legalism and harshness to which it is always open, and which often issue in the complete breakdown of discipline. Furthermore, to understand church discipline as brotherly discipline is to move away from the debates, often sterile, about the authority of elders which are a feature of modern discussion. Whilst the Anabaptist churches did recognise the gift of eldership, and placed great store by it, they refused to confine the exercise of discipline to elders. Brotherly discipline is the discipline of the brotherhood. That is to say, it involves the whole church, each member having a responsibility to care for every other member.

According to Menno, the key of binding, which is "nothing but the Word and the righteousness of God: the directing, commanding, threatening, terrifying, condemning Law of the Lord. . .", is "given to his ministers *and* people. . ."[31] When the ban is exercised, it is the work of the whole church undertaken in the fear of God. The unrepentant brother "is brought before the congregation" which has "the judging Word of the Scriptures, by which they may expel him and announce to him by the

88

Spirit of Christ that he is now no longer a member of the body of Christ. . ."[32] Even when this final stage has been reached, the church, though acting in judgment, does not cease to act in love, for the ban has been "ordained with a view to repentance and not to destruction".[33]

Thirdly, as I have already remarked, the Anabaptists viewed church discipline as a process. Following Matthew 18:15-17 they regarded the first stages of fraternal admonition as secret. The wronged brother does not go either to the elders or to the church but to the erring brother, and seeks to win him to amendment of life. Should this fail he still persists in seeking to win his brother, but this time he does so in the presence of witnesses, who are necessary if the matter should unfortunately not be settled at this second stage. The witnesses may presumably be elders, though this is not stated. The next stage involves going before the church, the whole brotherhood. Should the brother still refuse to listen to the church, he is to be expelled—"let him be to you as a Gentile and a tax collector".[34]

Menno, unfortunately, followed the Vulgate translation of "tax-collectors" as "publicani". He renders it very literally as "public, or manifest sinners". I say unfortunately, because it seems to me that here we possibly have the source of a tension which developed in Menno's thinking towards the end of his life, when he was being pressed by "hard-liners" (such as Leonard Bouwens) who were extremely rigorous in the use of the ban. Bouwens employed the ban without preliminary examination in most cases. There are even instances where the elders, or those commissioned by them, entered the house of an adulterous husband by night and forcibly removed his protesting wife and screaming children in enforcement of the ban.[35]

In his earlier writing on the subject of church discipline, Menno had argued that the process laid down in Matthew 18:15-17 should be applied to every sin. Later he modified this position, maintaining that for certain notorious and public sins "the rule of three admonitions"[36] should be dispensed with on the ground "that men may not return those whom God himself by his Spirit and Word excludes, lest Christ and his church be divided from each other".[37]

The dangers of Menno's position are obvious. Firstly, it implies there are certain sins which fall outside of the possibility of fraternal admonition and demand immediate action in the excommunication of the offender. While it is true that the New Testament does appear to make a distinction between forgivable and unforgivable sin (see Mk. 3:29; 1 John 5:16; 1 Cor. 5:11) yet, as Marlin Jeschke has recently pointed out, an invalid conclusion is drawn. "It infers that a certain class of sins *per se* indicate a fall from grace and therefore an individual's response to the gospel can be prejudged. In the case of this given class of sins the invitation to repentance can then be by-passed as unnecessary, for in effect these sins are by definition unforgivable. The corollary inference is that another class of sins is tolerable in that they do not necessitate excommunication. The tendency to classify sins generally leads to the toleration of some sinners in the church".[38] He goes on to say, to my mind rightly, that "Church discipline is called for by sin as such, and sin is any act or spirit inconsistent with the discipled life. Often this may not even be connected with so-called grave sins; for discipline may be occasioned by a person's coldness of heart and neglect of Christian fellowship, and it may be rendered unnecessary in the case of so-called grave sins that are followed immediately by repentance and therefore do not signify a fall from grace".[39] Whilst it would be unfair to Menno to suggest that he himself would have wished to argue to this conclusion, it is certainly fair to say that by distinguishing between "manifest sinners" and others he opened the door to the idea that some sins, being more heinous than others, require a more rigid discipline than lesser sins.

The second danger of Menno's position is that by dispensing with the stages of fraternal admonition, it opens the door to the unbridled exercise of power by determined men who occupy places of leadership. Thus, the afore-mentioned Leonard Bouwens banned the leaders of the moderate faction in the churches of Franeker and Emden, not because of their sins, but because they could not agree with his rigorous interpretation of the ban as involving separation in "bed and board" when a spouse was excommunicated. The eventual result of Bouwens' "hard-line" was the Waterlander schism.[40] It is surely significant, too, that most schisms among the Mennonites have been over the use of the ban.

The fourth feature of Anabaptist church discipline to which I wish to draw attention is the ban. The term is used to denote either exclusion from communion (kleiner Bann), or exclusion from membership (grosser Bann), though, as far as I can see, Menno did not make this distinction, which appears to have been made at a later stage of Mennonite history.[41]

From the beginning of their history the ban was practised in Anabaptist churches. The introduction of the ban was one of the principal demands at Zurich.

The ban replaces the death penalty prescribed in the Old Testament. It is the Church's last resort, for it has no other weapon. The erring brother is not to be handed over to the civil authorities for physical punishment, yet his dismissal from the church is solemn and severe. According to Menno the apostolic ban "is a delivering over to Satan, yes, a public expulsion, excommunication, or separation from the congregation, church, body, and Kingdom of Christ, and that in the name of Christ, with the binding power of the Holy Ghost and the Word".[42] How seriously banning was viewed, and perhaps an indication of why it was carried out only after a day spent in prayer and fasting, may be appreciated by reflecting upon another statement of Menno: "It is incontrovertible that all who are outside of the congregation and church of Christ must be in that of Antichrist."[43]

The erring brother is expelled, in the last analysis, because he has already separated from Christ. It is inconceivable that he can therefore remain any longer within the body of Christ, the church. Excommunication thus formally seals what has already taken place—separation from Christ. Menno goes so far as to say that "no one is excommunicated or expelled by us from the communion of the brethren but those who have already separated and expelled themselves from Christ's communion either by false doctrine or by improper conduct".[44]

After the ban has been carried out, the excommunicated person was shunned or avoided. All contact with him was to be avoided unless a work of mercy was indicated, for example, caring for him if he were ill. The scriptural basis for shunning was found in Matthew 18:17 and 1 Corinthians 5:11. As the pious Jews would allow themselves no contact with Gentiles or tax-collectors, so the Church should have no dealings with the banned member.[45]

How far should shunning be carried? What should happen if a husband were excommunicated? Should his wife, as a member of the church, avoid all contact with him, in terms both of "bed and board"? Menno and the more rigorous of the Anabaptists argued that there could be no exceptions to the rule. "If some liberty should be granted to some, it would be more reasonable to give the whole church liberty to eat and deal with apostates than to give it to husband and wife. For it can do this with less danger than husbands and wives who are continuously together, something which the church could easily avoid."[46] Furthermore, there is the argument from experience. "I have known not much less than three hundred spouses in my day who did not observe between them and their mates the ordinance, counsel, doctrine, will and command of the Lord and his apostles concerning shunning, and have so run together into perdition."[47]

Other Anabaptists, particularly in the Rhineland and in Switzerland, took a more liberal view of shunning, being prepared to allow that enforced separation would serve rather to harden than to humble the erring member. The issue of the extent of the ban was to prove a fruitful source of division; a number of schisms have resulted in consequence of one party insisting on a rigorous line whilst others have pleaded for a more tolerant application of the principle of shunning. Though the more liberal view is predominant today, shunning in "bed and board" continues to be practised among the Old Order Amish and Old Colony Mennonites, and some other groups.[48]

iv Issues arising from the Exercise of Church Discipline

A study of Anabaptist church discipline raises, it seems to me, several important issues.

Firstly, there is the difficulty of avoiding legalism on the one hand and laxity on the other.

If one maintains, on scriptural grounds, the regenerate nature of the church there is always the danger that the church's separation from the world will be understood more in terms of taboos which have to be maintained than in terms of free and responsible Christian discipleship. For example, during the sixteenth century men, in general, wore beards. During the seventeenth century they shaved, and there was some objection to this practice in Mennonite congregations. Once shaving was accepted, it was difficult again to change to a beard when it returned to popularity.[49]

On the other hand, fear of legalism can lead to laxity about the whole matter of church discipline. In later Mennonite history, especially as far as Germany and Russia are concerned, discipline virtually disappeared. Clearly it is one thing to identify legalism and seek to avoid it. It is quite another to deal with laxity. How does one preserve the tension between the freedom into which grace brings the believer and the responsible and ordered discipleship to which the regenerated believer is committed? How does one draw the line between legalism and a proper concern for the purity of the church? How does one distinguish between charitable tolerance and un-Christian laxity? These are not easy questions to answer, but they are important enough to be pondered carefully.

Secondly, there is the problem of what can be called the "second generation". G. H. Williams has argued that, between 1540-1557, the Anabaptists were using the ban and the equally formalised solemn reinstatement into membership as "the ethical and constitutional equivalent of believer's baptism for the increasingly numerous 'birthright' members, who in routinized baptism in adolescence were no longer undergoing the great formative experience of the public *re*baptism of the heroic days of the first apostles of the new evangel".[50] Even if Williams is overstating the problem for the period 1540-1557, he is nonetheless rightly identifying the major problem which faces gathered churches—that of staying gathered. Routinized baptism in adolescence is not peculiar to Anabaptist congregations; we recognise the same phenomenon among the Welsh Baptists and, at a much earlier age, in the Southern Baptist churches of the United States.

When an increasing number of "birthright" members (those brought up in the church) are admitted, is there a tendency to make discipline more rigorous in an attempt to maintain a high level of discipleship, or is a point soon reached when discipline begins to fall into disuse because the "birthright" outlook becomes predominant? How can the problem of the "second generation" be dealt with, unless by continuous schisms caused by ardent spirits whose answer to laxity is to form new, pure churches, which in a generation or two exhibit the same features as the bodies from which they have seceded. This is not an academic question, but a severely practical one which has to be faced by today's separatists if they do not wish to become tomorrow's conformists.

Thirdly, there is the pressing issue of authority. Where does the authority for church discipline lie? Is it with the elders, as some, following John Owen, not too accurately I fear, would maintain? Does it lie with the church? If so, could not this work against church discipline being exercised, particularly when a fair proportion of members are related to one another?

We have already noticed the tension within Anabaptist thinking between the rigorists, who tended to stress the authority of the eldership, and the more tolerant party, which maintained that the three admonitions should apply to all offences. The same tension exists among us today. There are those who emphasise the eldership, and those who emphasise the church, as the seat of authority. Probably the truth lies at neither extreme. May it be that we shall have to think in terms of the authority of both spiritually qualified and ecclesiastically recognised leadership *and* the whole body of the church? If that is the case, the problem of authority requires re-definition: it is the problem of defining the relationship between leadership and community. As in national life a government can lose credibility, so in the life of a church the eldership can come to the position of lacking any living authority. Yet, on the other hand, as a community can suffer because it either lacks or will not recognise leadership, so can a church. Is there not a sense in which, when there is a properly functioning spiritual organism, the problem of authority is not an issue, because the leadership is sensitive to the rest of the body and the body accepts the leadership? If so, what happens when the leadership and the body are out of harmony? How can harmony be restored so that the organism functions properly once again?

If writers like Menno Simons do not supply us with easy answers to our questions, they do at least enable us to identify some of our problems, as we regard the ways in which they wrestled to rebuild the walls of separation which marked the Church from the world.

v   The Relevance of Anabaptist Thinking for our day

I have been struck by the contemporary ring of the Anabaptist material on the subject of church discipline. Various reasons can be suggested, I think, to account for this.

Firstly, the Anabaptists were seeking to re-establish the Church life and order which they had discovered in the New Testament. To do so, they had to challenge the "system", whether Roman, Lutheran, Zwinglian or Calvinist version of it. They were consciously a minority group with the big battalions ranged against them. They were not deterred, however for they had an unbounded confidence in the power of God's Word and the power of God's Spirit.

Our situation today is not unlike theirs. The big battalions are not on our side. As far as establishment evangelicals are concerned, we scarcely exist. Let us be possessed of the same vision as our Anabaptist forebears. Without pride or censorious legalism let us seek, like them, to re-establish, through the Word of God and by the power of the Spirit, the church life and order of the New Testament.

Secondly, we can learn from their mistakes. Some of the Anabaptists fell into the pit of legalism, others fell into the slough of laxity. As John had to contend with a Diotrephes so there were men like Leonard Bouwens, who loved power so much that he embittered the closing years of Menno's life and eventually thrust him out of leadership. I suggest that we need to be on our guard, lest we repeat too easily the mistakes and excesses of our forebears.

Thirdly, we need to recover the Anabaptist emphasis on the church as a brotherhood. We have accepted, without question, the unbiblical individualism which has characterised evangelication for far too long. Thus, the church is viewed as a kind of spiritual petrol station at which one gets "filled up" for the week but as for relationship with other members of the body of Christ—there is none! To view the church as a brotherhood, and to apply this concept practically, is to behave quite differently. When we accept that we are brothers then we relate to each other in the dynamics of personal relationships, and give ourselves to one another in a love patterned upon the love of Him who gave Himself for the church.[51] Then truly the church becomes "the society of those who care" for one another, and for mankind.

REFERENCES

[1]G. H. Williams: *A People in Community—Historical Background*, in James Les Garrett Jr. (editor), *The Concept of the Believers' Church*, Herald Press, Scottdale, Penn., U.S.A., 1969, p. 101.

[2]The problems of the evidence are frequently overlooked by popular writers such as E. H. Broadbent, *The Pilgrim Church*, who assert that there has been a continuing line of believers' churches from the first century through the Middle Ages to the Reformation and beyond to the present day.

[3]Quoted by R. H. Bainton, *Studies in the Reformation*, Hodder & Stoughton, London, 1964, pp. 41-42.

[4]Quoted by J. Lecler, *Toleration and Reformation* (E. T.) 2 vols., 1960, I, p. 316.

[5]*The Complete Writings of Menno Simons* (Scottdale, 1956), p. 679, quoted Harold S. Bender: "The Anabaptist Vision" in Guy F. Herschberger (ed.); *The Recovery of the Anabaptist Vision*, Herald Press, Scottdale, Penn., U.S.A., p. 48.

[6]Quoted by G. H. Williams, *The Radical Reformation*, London and New York, 1962, pp. 122-3.

[7]This account of Menno's early life is based on H. S. Bender: "A Brief Biography of Menno Simons," pp. 4-14 in J. C. Wanger (ed.), *The Complete Writings of Menno Simons*, Scottdale, 1956.

[8]W. L. Lumpkin (ed.); *Baptist Confessions of Faith*, Judson Press, U.S.A., 1959, p. 19.

[9]Herschberger, op. cit., p. 42.

[10]William Klassen; *Covenant and Community—The Life and Writings of Pilgram Marpeck*, Eerdmans, Grand Rapids, U.S.A., 1968, p. 21.

11*Writings*, pp. 410-11. 12Ibid, p. 413. 13Quoted H. S. Bender in Herschberger (ed.), p. 44. 14H. S. Bender, op. cit., p. 43, No. 28. 15Bender, ibid, p. 43.

16The adverb "probably" has to be used as it is possible that the homily from which this quotation is taken *Von dem geheimnus der tauf*, is a composite work by Thomas Münzier and Hans Hut. See the discussion in Rollin Stely Armour, *Anabaptist Baptism*, Herald Press, 1966, pp. 57-75.

17Quoted Armour, op. cit., p. 69. 18Harold S. Bender, op. cit., p. 47. 19Ibid., p. 50. 20Armour, op. cit., p. 144. 21Bender, op. cit., p. 53. 22Cited Bender, op. cit., p. 51. 23Mennonite Encyclopaedia, I, p. 219.

24Quoted L. Verduin, *The Reformers and Their Step-Children*, British edition, 1966, Paternoster Press, Exeter, p. 120, n.

25Quoted L. Verduin, ibid, p. 125. Taken from Calvin's refutation of the Anabaptist manifesto published at Schlattan am Raude, (1527), printed in C. R., Vol. XXXV.

26Menno Simons, *Writings*, p. 725, quoting the words of his opponent, Gellins Faber, a former R.C. priest, who became the Protestant pastor in Emden, E. Friesland. In 1552 he published a bitter attack on the Anabaptists to which Menno Simons replied.

27*Writings*, p. 962. 28*Writings*, p. 457. 29*Writings*, p. 962. 30*Writings*, p. 413. 31*Writings*, p. 989, (my italics). 32*Writings*, p. 991. 33*Writings*, p. 470. 34*Writings*, p.459. 35G. H. Williams, op. cit., p. 494. 36"Reply to Sylis and Lemke" (1560), *Writings*, p. 1003, cf. p. 975. 37Ibid, p. 1003. 38Martin Jeschke, *Disciplining the Brother*, Herald Press, U.S.A., 1972, p. 661. 39Ibid, p. 73. 40G. H. Williams, op. cit., pp. 495-6. See also A. L. E. Verheyden, *Anabaptism in Flanders*, 1530-1560, Herald Press, U.S.A., E.T. 1961, p. 9. "The brotherhood of the Northern Netherlands was soon divided under the influence of the individualism of the elders desirous of leadership. . ."

41Art. "Ban", Mennonite Encyclopaedia, I, pp. 219-223. 42*Writings*, p. 967. 43Ibid, p. 967. 44Ibid, p. 415. 45Ibid, p. 459. 46Ibid, p. 1007. 47Ibid, p. 972. 48*Studies in Church Discipline*, Mennonite Publication Office, Newton, Kansas, U.S.A., 1958, p. 68. 49Ibid, p. 72. 50G. H. Williams, op. cit., p. 485. 51Eph. 5: 25.